THE STORY OF COLE YOUNGER

THE STORY OF
COLE YOUNGER

by HIMSELF

BEING AN AUTOBIOGRAPHY
OF THE MISSOURI GUERRILLA CAPTAIN AND OUTLAW,
HIS CAPTURE AND PRISON LIFE,
AND THE ONLY AUTHENTIC ACCOUNT
OF THE NORTHFIELD RAID EVER PUBLISHED

Introduction by
MARLEY BRANT

MINNESOTA HISTORICAL SOCIETY PRESS

Original edition published by the Press of the Henneberry Company, Chicago, 1903

www.mhspress.org

The Minnesota Historical Society Press is a member of the Association of American University Presses.

Manufactured in the United States of America

10 9 8 7 6 5 4 3

♾ The paper used in this publication meets the minimum requirements of the American National Standard for Information Sciences—Permanence for Printed Library Materials, ANSI Z39.48-1984.

International Standard Book Number
ISBN 13: 978-0-87351-393-7 (paper)
ISBN 10: 0-87351-393-2 (paper)

Cataloging-in-Publication Data on file at the Library of Congress

PICTURE CREDITS

The items pictured are from the collections of the Minnesota Historical Society, St. Paul, except the following illustrations reproduced from the Henneberry Company edition: Cole Younger (frontispiece and back cover), Bob Younger, Jim Younger, John Younger, Nannie Harris and Charity Kerr, William Clarke Quantrill, John Jarrette, William H. Gregg, Jesse James, Frank James, and Wild West show advertisement.

Contents

Illustrations

Bob Younger (above), *Jim Younger*
(above right), *John Younger* (right)

*Cole Younger's cousins
Nannie Harris and
Charity Kerr (who
was killed in the
wreck of the Kansas
City guard house)*

William Clarke Quantrill,
the Confederate guerrilla leader

John Jarrette, Cole Younger's
brother-in-law and fellow
guerrilla with Quantrill

William H. Gregg,
fellow guerrilla

Jesse James
(top)

Frank James
(bottom)

Northfield, Minnesota, looking east into Bridge Square, ca. 1876 (by Sumner Studio, Northfield). On the right, the north front of the Scriver Block building (where the First National Bank is located) faces the square.

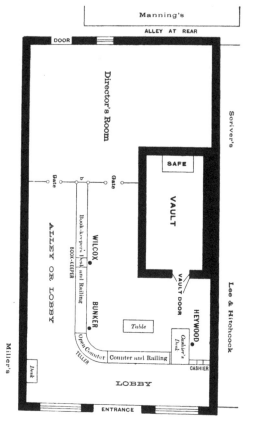

Manning's

ALLEY AT REAR

DOOR

Director's Room

Scriver's

SAFE

VAULT

Gate

b

Gate

Book-keeper's Desk and Railing

BOOK-KEEPER

WILCOX

ALLEY OR LOBBY

BUNKER

VAULT DOOR

Lee & Hitchcock

Table

HEYWOOD

Open Counter

TELLER

Counter and Railing

Cashier's Desk

CASHIER

Miller's

Desk

LOBBY

ENTRANCE

Diagram of interior of the bank, which shows the positions at the beginning of the raid of bank employees Joseph Lee Heywood, Alonzo E. Bunker, and Frank J. Wilcox (from Robber and Hero, by George Huntington)

The raid on the First National Bank of Northfield
on September 7, 1876, as freely imagined by an artist
for The Northfield Tragedy, by J. H. Hanson

THE FIGHT IN THE STREETS OF NORTHFIELD BETWEEN THE ROBBERS AND CITIZENS.

The entrance to the First National Bank correctly appears in the center right in this illustration from The Northfield Tragedy.

The posse that captured the Younger brothers. From left to right: Sheriff James Glispin, Capt. William W. Murphy, George A. Bradford, Benjamin M. Rice, Col. Thomas L. Vought, Charles A. Pomeroy, and S. J. Severson.

Robbers and citizens. Clockwise, from top:
murdered cashier Joseph Lee Heywood, Sheriff James Glispin, robbers Bob
Younger, Charley Pitts, Jim Younger, and Cole Younger, citizen "August Suborn"
(a pseudonym of Asle Oscar Sorbel). Center: robbers "Bill Chadwell" (pseudo-
nym of Bill Stiles) and Clell (or Clel) Miller. Following the raid, Ira E. Sumner of
Northfield photographed the bodies of Pitts, Chadwell, and Miller; grouping of
photographs by photographer William H. Jacoby, Minneapolis.

Cole (right), Jim, and Bob (left) Younger with their sister Henrietta, photographed in Stillwater prison two weeks before Bob's death in 1889 (by J. M. Kuhn, Stillwater)

Cole Younger in the general population uniform worn by most prisoners, probably shortly after being committed in November, 1876, to the Minnesota State Prison in Stillwater

The Prison Mirror

Lew. P. Schoonmaker, - - Editor.
LLOYD PORTER, AND THOMAS CLARK
Compositors.
COLE YOUNGER, "Printer's Devil"

Prison Locals.
————— :O: —————

—Receiver R. S. Brown paid us $10.00 for the first printed copy of THE MIRROR.

—The stone steps leading into the new main cell building is a great improvement.

—Mrs. J. S. Anderson of the city of Stillwater, was the first subscriber to THE PRISON MIRROR

—There are three bubbling springs in the prison yard which supply the entire prison with pure, clear water.

—The prisoners will do well to observe closely, the rules governing the prison library, which will appear in our next issue.

—Behold, in this wicked world many good Threshing Machines are made, of which, the Machine Made here is "Chief."

—Twenty eight sacks of flour, of 100 lbs. each, and 100 lbs. of corn meal is used each week in preparing the "staff of life" for our prison population.

—The friends of THE MIRROR, will be confering a favor upon us, by patronizing those generous merchants whose advertisements appear in our columns.

—Stewart Benner is to have a new kitchen built and other improvements to facilitate the preparation of food, among which is steam for cooking purposes.

—Officer W. Wells, has gone out to his farm near Janesville, on a months vacation, he did not forget to subscribe for THE MIRROR however, before he went.

—Warden Stordock has provided our prison choir with a goodly supply of handsome new hymn books, and the boys are furnishing us now with some excellent singing.

—An itemized statement of all receipts and expenditures in connection with this institution will in the future be published in THE MIRROR, the first Wednesday of each month.

—The "boys" occupying quarters opposite THE MIRROR office are delighted with the window which the Warden has had cut through the four foot walls to admit air and light into their heretofore dark, close and gloomy abodes.

—THE PRISON MIRROR, is for sale in the City of Burlington & Wilsons; at the Prison, at the Wardens office, also at the Editorial rooms, at 5 cents per copy. Subscriptions will also be taken at any of the above places at our regular rates, $1.00 per year.

—The following poem is respectfully dedicated to night officer William Hall, by our prison poet.

Oh, ye night guards often times make us
Feel like swearing a big swore,
When ye, tramping leave behind thee
Footprints on our painted floor.

—Cole Younger, our genial prison Librarian, has received new honors at the hands of THE MIRROR by being appointed to the honorable position of "printer devil" in which he will in the future keep the flies off all the gifts of "wedding cake," and other editorial favors of like nature which may find lodgement in our sanctum sanctorum.

While in Stillwater, Cole Younger helped to found its still-active newspaper. The premier issue of August 10, 1887, declared "'The Prison Mirror' casts its first reflections upon the world. And Sheds a ray of light upon the lives of those behind the bars" while identifying Younger as the "'Printer's Devil.'"

Introduction

COLE YOUNGER. The very name invokes a wide variety of vivid images: rugged, rough rider soldiering in the service of the diabolical William Clarke Quantrill; fearless train and bank robber with Jesse and Frank James; and misunderstood, repentant old man. Words such as vengeful, honorable, intelligent, jovial, and egotistical also attach themselves to the man.

In my twenty-plus years of studying Younger, I have been continuously intrigued with the many sides of this sometimes imperious, other times acquiescent, unique frontier personality. I find that Cole exhibited a multitude of dispositions, each directed toward the objective at hand. This was a strong-willed man who wanted what he wanted when he wanted it, and employed any means to reach his goal. He was at times forceful, driven, and antagonistic. Yet he could easily turn on the charm and impel even his strongest enemies to view him as humble, powerless, and penitent. Chameleon-like, Cole adapted himself to whatever light best suited his needs and desires. During his tempestuous youth, he learned all the tricks and paid more than a premium price to achieve his ultimate goal. Cole Younger, like his comrade and adversary Jesse James, would never have settled for anything less than what he felt he deserved: legendary status.

Exactly who was Thomas Coleman Younger, the notorious outlaw? Born in 1844 Cole, along with his thirteen brothers and sisters, was descended from two well-known Southern families. His parents, Henry and Bursheba Fristoe Younger, fared well during the first twenty-some years of marriage. They owned at least

two farms in Jackson County, Missouri, and were considered
wealthy and socially prominent. This would change with the on-
sets of the Kansas-Missouri border war in 1857 and the War between the States in 1861. The dry-goods store owned by Henry
Younger would be robbed continuously by both Kansas Jayhawkers and Redlegs. His adored son Richard would die from an
illness at the early age of twenty-one, and Henry himself would
be ambushed and murdered by Union soldiers.

Having been forced, if only in his own mind, into the back-
ground due to the educational and business achievements of his
eldest brother, Cole was determined to prove that he was every
bit as capable and promising as brother Richard. He developed
the disposition of a happy, educated, devil-may-care arbiter of
good taste and good humor. Girls adored him, and the young
men of the area always included him in their adventures, as Cole
could be counted on to provide a good time. Not many people
were aware of his darker side—that of a rebellious and obstinate
bully. This was the side that Cole's younger brothers Jim, John,
and Bob, grew to know and resent. Cole would eventually prove
his worth at great cost, and his brothers would ultimately be en-
veloped in his need to make a grandiose statement of his worth.

With the full outbreak of the War between the States, Cole
realized that he was a born soldier. Not just any soldier, but one
who, through his superior intellect, cunning, and insight, would
be noticed and glorified. Enlisting with the ruthless Missouri
Confederate guerrillas at the age of seventeen, Cole quickly became a successful disciple of William Clarke Quantrill, their
barbarous leader. His combat techniques were honed, and his
approach to difficult strategic situations was admired by those
in charge. Cole rapidly rose to the position of "captain" and
made a name for himself at the battle of Lone Jack, Missouri, as
a fair and compassionate adversary. Before long he had earned
the reputation he desired. His name was placed near the top of
the guerrilla hierarchy, known by all who favored the move-

ment and, with caution and disdain, by those who did not. Cole became what he had always hoped to be: a regional hero.

After the war Cole found that, although he continued to be well respected by supporters of the Lost Cause, he was labeled an outlaw by the Union government. Unable to return to local society, Cole could not enjoy the reputation he had earned. He did not like that turn of events one bit. Nor did he like the conquering society that robbed him of both freedom and glory. During the war Cole had become close friends with Frank James, a fellow guerrilla under Quantrill. When Frank suggested that Cole join him and his brother Jesse in an event guaranteed to restore their hard-won reputations as men of action, while at the same time rewarding them with vast sums of money, Cole was quick to enlist in yet another organization: the James-Younger gang. After his first robbery, there was no turning back for Cole Younger.

Bearing in mind that Cole had found glory in the days when he was a soldier and seeker of justice, it is not surprising that he would bathe his activities in this resplendent light for the rest of his days. With the biased righteousness of the defeated and humiliated, Cole continually sought retribution for the wrongs committed against him. No matter the victory or the defeat, Cole always saw himself as the victim of an unjust society. Little that he did could not be justified in his own mind. And such would be the approach when he decided to set the record straight and write his life's story, first published in 1903.

Whether Cole Younger was a master storyteller, or simply in denial about most of his illegal activities, is debatable. I suppose there are even those who, more than one hundred years after the outlaw's Waterloo, believe his statement that the Northfield, Minnesota, bank raid of 1876 was the only robbery in which he participated. Since Cole was not tried for any other crime, the truth will never be known about all the robberies that he may have committed. He denied living a life outside of the law from the onset of the criminal career that biographers believe he indeed lived. From the time of the first robbery that he was suspected of having a hand in, the raid on the Clay County Savings Association in Liberty, Missouri, on February 13, 1866, Cole told some mighty tall tales.

By 1903 Cole Younger had served twenty-five years in the Minnesota State Prison in Stillwater, paying his debt to society for his participation in the Northfield affair. He had been paroled in 1901 and pardoned in February 1903. The list of Cole's suspected crimes, which he denied having had anything to do with, was as long as his arm. With the editorial assistance of his late-life, good friend (and future Jackson County Marshal) Harvey C. ("Harry") Hoffman, and financial aid from other friends and family members, Cole had decided to compose the story of his life. At least it would be the story of his life that Cole would have his readers believe.

The Story of Cole Younger by Himself is subtitled *Being an Autobiography of the Missouri Guerrilla Captain and Outlaw, His Capture and Prison Life, and the Only Authentic Account of the Northfield Raid Ever Published.* In his preface Cole claims that he will use the book to offset with truth the lies told by "sensationalists." He concludes "I wish to say that from cover to cover there is not a statement which could not be verified." During more than two decades of intense study of Cole Younger, the James brothers, and their families, I have found little to support Cole's conspicuously stated objective to tell the whole truth and nothing but the truth. Cole, like his partner-in-crime Jesse James, uses the power of the printed word to deny his wrongdoings and elevate himself into a misunderstood, if not honorable, war hero and protector of truth, justice, women, children, and the American way.

Cole begins his book by discussing in detail the prestigious family from whence he came. This is probably the most truthful chapter of his account, although other members of his extended family tree may have been horrified to find their ancestry linked to his in so public a manner. Also notable is Cole's reminisce of his wartime activities, which, while playing up his participation and seeking quiet glory for his multitudinous acts of chivalry, reads like very creative fiction. The events in Cole's war reminisce likely did occur, but the accuracy of his description remains elusive to documentation.

The fact that Cole, as a guerrilla, and his family, as unwilling participants in the horrific life of Confederate civilians, led lives of uncertainty, anxiety, and turmoil cannot be ignored. The war in Missouri was bitter and brutal, regardless of which side any given resident favored. The Younger family suffered greatly. Whether Cole was justified in seeking retribution and a certain protection for his family through his alliance with Quantrill is arguable, but he does seem sincere in his belief this was the only path that he could take. Special times create special circumstances, and perhaps it was appropriate for Cole to seek whatever means he could to provide some degree of succor for his widowed mother and younger siblings.

Cole's report of the massacre at Lawrence, Kansas, is probably fairly accurate, from a guerrilla's point of view. It is also likely that, as he states, Cole did save some lives. He was known not to be brutal in battle. It has been documented elsewhere that he was considered by both comrades and foes as a fair and reasonable soldier, often sparing lives or seeing that enemies were appropriately treated. Throughout his career, Cole Younger was not a savage man. He often went out of his way to avoid fatal physical confrontations and used his gun against others only as a last resort.

Yet by the time that Cole arrives at the chapters of his book about his outlaw days, his capricious way with a phrase rapidly metamorphoses into fantasy. If we are to believe Cole, he was never involved in any robbery except Northfield and knew the James brothers primarily through his wartime associations. The description by Cole of his first meeting with Jesse James raises the immediate suspicion that all is not truthful in this book. Cole claims to have met Jesse at a post-war gathering of former guerrillas who had participated in the Lawrence raid and had responded to an attorney claiming that he could defend their actions in a court of law.

Such a gathering has not been documented. Even if the meeting took place, it is extremely unlikely that Jesse James attended since he was not at Lawrence and was, in fact, still recovering from a near-fatal wartime wound at the time. It is more likely that Cole met Jesse through his close friend Frank James after the Jameses had made plans to rob the Clay County Savings Association and Frank sought to include Cole in this foray.

Cole says that he was in St. Clair County, Missouri, at the time of the robbery at Russellville, Kentucky. (He would claim to have been at the homes of family and friends in this area almost every time he was suspected of participating in a robbery.) There is some truth to his being often in the St. Clair area, but it is likely that he was there either before or after the robberies—which he probably committed—in order to line up alibis and establish his being there about that time. His claim to have been in Louisiana during the Savannah and Richmond robberies in Missouri is true. This alibi would give credence to the others, in Cole's mind. Cole implies that if one of his alibis is valid, *all* of them are.

Throughout the book, Cole also provides alibis for his brothers, implying that if these alibis are valid he should, in turn, also be let off the hook. Jim Younger would likely not have been happy with Cole's approach, as it is questionable whether Jim participated in any robbery other than Northfield. John, on the other hand, actually was in California at the time specified by Cole in regard to the Corydon, Iowa, robbery, as he had yet to join the gang. The same holds true for Bob, who, no doubt, was living as a sixteen-year-old boy with his family in Dallas at the time of that same robbery and would not join the gang for several more years.

As close as Cole claimed to be to his brothers, he was not above using them to elevate his own status or divert blame away from himself. Poor brother Bob would later take the brunt of the responsibility for the Northfield fiasco. He would also serve to demonstrate Cole's generosity and fabled name. Cole writes that he paid for Bob to attend college, and states that Bob left because he could not escape Cole's infamy. No records have been located confirming Bob's attendance at William and Mary. Because of the War between the States, Bob went to school for only a few years, and entering college would have been an unlikely feat for him. Besides, Cole's vast fame at the time seems to be a figment of Cole's imagination. It would be years before the name Cole Younger was so widely known. Cole was the first to connect brother John with a robbery when he mentioned him in an alibi for the Kansas City fair heist. The public then was not aware that John Younger even existed.

Because of the blatant lies in Cole's autobiography, it is hard to know when he is telling the truth. In the case of his association with Belle Starr, however, he may well be reliable. The young Myra Shirley no doubt was enamored of the guerrilla captain, but that is probably as far as things went. The identity of the father of Belle's daughter, who would later be called Pearl Younger, is controversial. I believe that Cole, as he states, was not Pearl's father.

All and all, Cole's stories about his post-war activities must be viewed with more than a grain of salt. He has interwoven a handful of true adventures with fictitious tales about being wrongly accused of numerous robberies by law enforcement and the public. These stories all portray Cole as a harassed cattle driver whose only purpose in life is to protect his family and live as best a life he can after having been unjustly labeled an outlaw. He accords little thought to the possibility that his protests of innocence have given critics all the more reason to believe that his family members were more intimately involved in his life of crime.

Cole continues his account with great emphasis on the robbery at Northfield. Again, he takes literary license to tell a story of misadventure, misjudgment, and mismanagement, interspersed with some truths about the gang's Minnesota travels before the robbery. Cole begins by saying that, because of all of the robberies that were "laid at our doors," he and his brothers decided to execute their first and only robbery so that they could escape their persecutors once and for all. Then they would relocate to South America, where they would no longer be unjustly accused of crimes.

Throughout his narrative of the Northfield fiasco, Cole refers to two accomplices as Howard and Woods. He adamantly refuses to name Jesse and Frank James as his partners-in-crime. It is interesting that the Jameses are given aliases so close to the names that they used while posing as upright citizens in Tennessee. Jesse was known there as Tom Howard and Frank as Ben Woodson. Cole would always state emphatically that Jesse and Frank had nothing to do with Northfield. It seems, however, that he could not find it within himself to be creative enough to assign the brothers names far different from those that would be later identified as ones they had used in the Nashville area. Perhaps Cole subconsciously, or pointedly, found it difficult to maintain the oath of silence upon which he and the James brothers had agreed.Cole relates the story of the gang's pre-robbery days with a rare bit of truthfulness. No fool, he had to know that these stories could and would be substantiated by eyewitnesses. He sets us up correctly for the immediate event of the robbery, but the story as to consequence and blame deteriorates into one that I, at least, have a great deal of difficulty believing. Cole tells us that his brother Bob, whom Cole had never known before to drink, joined Howard and Pitts in consuming a quart of whiskey. This seems quite unlikely.

Even if the inexperienced, young Bob were to have gotten drunk for the first time immediately before committing a complicated robbery, there are other factors that make this dubious. I have concluded that it was not Charlie Pitts but Frank James who was the third outlaw inside the bank during the robbery. While Jesse was known to imbibe the occasional glass of wine or social drink, it is extremely unlikely that the experienced Frank would allow either himself or his partners-in-crime to become drunk. The robberies of the James-Younger gang were planned with precision. To think that a robbery in unknown territory would not be taken seriously is to ignore the characters of the individual gang members.

In this book, Cole says that he did not know until after the robbery was over that the men had been drinking. In later accounts he said that he knew, but could not stop it. The idea of Cole Younger being a powerless bystander is ridiculous. Had Cole believed that the men were drunk, he would have demanded that the robbery be called off, at the very least. This cover-up is clearly intended to hold him blameless. Cole's information, which we can conjecture as mostly untrue, was presented after the deaths of brother Bob (who died in prison of consumption in 1889) and Charlie Pitts, who was killed by the posse at the scene of the Youngers' surrender at Hanska Slough in 1876.

Cole undoubtedly places Pitts in the bank to substitute him for Woods (Frank James) and keep Frank away from the scene of cashier Joseph Lee Heywood's murder. Careful study causes me to conclude that Frank James murdered Heywood. Frank can be placed inside the bank through physical descriptions by eyewitnesses. The dun horse, whose rider the contemporary press speculated was the man who shot Heywood, has been identified as a horse purchased and ridden by Frank James. Frank's own family believes that he was the murderer. Cole says that Frank and Jesse were not involved in the Northfield robbery because he and Jesse were not friends. That much is true: the two were often adversaries for the leadership of the gang, and their strong, egotistical personalities effectively sabotaged any efforts by Frank to create a more tranquil fraternity, but this does not remove guilt from the Jameses.

Cole correctly relates the events of the post-robbery man-hunt and the Youngers' eventual surrender at Hanska Slough. Again, the existence of dozens of eyewitness accounts prevents him from diverting too far from the true path. Cole's pages on life at Stillwater prison are innocuous enough, and the mentions of post-release activities seem mostly truthful. Cole veers from the path slightly while relating the story of his brother Jim's suicide, claiming that he did not take charge of Jim's remains only be-cause he was "sick in bed" at the time of Jim's death. The fact is that Cole and Jim were not friendly at the time, due to differ-ences of opinion over the way that Jim chose to conduct his life, especially his love life. Jim, an intelligent, sensitive man, re-sented, as had brother Bob, Cole's interference.

Cole uses his final pages to reprint the text from the lecture that he later delivered throughout the Midwest, "What My Life Has Taught Me." The Bryanesque delivery of life's lessons learned provides further insight into the man who was and who might have been. The story of Cole Younger, whose personality comprised the guises of victim, adventurer, redeemer, brother, friend, and fabricator, is a complicated tale. There was only one Cole Younger. This autobiography, told with all its truths, half-truths, insights, anecdotes, and outright lies, makes for an en-gaging and electrifying read. When all is said and done, Cole Younger—partly truth and partly fiction—is a captivating Amer-ican legend.

MARLEY BRANT
Atlanta, Ga.
April, 2000

Cole Younger was born near Lee's Summit, Missouri, on Jan-uary 15, 1844, and died near his birthplace on March 21, 1916.

THE STORY OF COLE YOUNGER

PUBLISHER'S NOTE
This edition includes new footnotes and the correction of obvious misspellings and typographical errors.

Why This Book Is Here

Many may wonder why an old "guerrilla" should feel called upon at this late day to rehearse the story of his life. On the eve of sixty, I come out into the world to find a hundred or more of books, of greater or less pretensions, purporting to be a history of "The Lives of the Younger Brothers," but which are all nothing more nor less than a lot of sensational recitals, with which the Younger brothers never had the least association. One publishing house alone is selling sixty varieties of these books, and I venture to say that in the whole lot there could not be found six pages of truth. The stage, too, has its lurid dramas in which we are painted in devilish blackness.

It is therefore my purpose to give an authentic and absolutely correct history of the lives of the "Younger Brothers," in order that I may, if possible, counteract in some measure at least, the harm that has been done my brothers and myself, by the blood and thunder accounts of misdeeds, with which relentless sensationalists have charged us, but which have not even the suggestion of truth about them, though doubtless they have had everything to do with coloring public opinion.

In this account I propose to set out the little good that was in my life, at the same time not withholding in any way the bad, with the hope of setting right before the world a family name once honored, but which has suffered disgrace by being charged with more evil deeds than were ever its rightful share.

To the host of friends in Minnesota and Missouri who have done everything possible to help my brother and myself during the last few years, with no other object than the love of doing good and aiding fellow creatures in suffering, I wish to say that I shall always conduct myself so that they will never have the least cause to regret having championed our cause, or feel any shame in the friendship so generously proven to us. Nothing lies deeper in my heart than the gratitude I feel to them all, except a desire to prove myself worthy.

In the two states named these friends are too numerous for me to mention each of their names, but among those in Missouri who traveled long journeys to Minnesota to plead my cause, even though they knew it to be unpopular in many quarters, I wish to especially thank Col. W. C. Bronough of Clinton, Capt. Steve Ragan, Colonel Rogers of Kansas City and Miss Cora MacNeill, now Mrs. George M. Bennett of Minneapolis, but also formerly of Kansas City.

In concluding these remarks, I wish to say that from cover to cover there is not a statement which could not be verified.

Yours truly,

COLE YOUNGER

Lee's Summit, Mo.

March, 1903

1

Boyhood Days

Political hatreds are always bitter, but none were ever more bitter than those which existed along the border line of Missouri and Kansas during my boyhood in Jackson county in the former state from 1856 to '60. These hatreds were soon to make trouble for me of which I had never dreamed.

Mine was a happy childhood. I was the seventh of fourteen children, but my father had prospered and we were given the best education the limited facilities of that part of the West then afforded.

My people had always been prominent, politically. It was born in the blood. My great grandmother on my father's side was a daughter of "Lighthorse Harry" Lee, whose proud memory we all cherish. The Youngers came from Strasburg, and helped to rule there when it was a free city. Henry Washington Younger, my father, represented Jackson county three times in the legislature, and was also judge of the county court. My mother, who was Bursheba Fristoe of Independence, was the daughter of Richard Fristoe who fought under General Andrew Jackson at New Orleans, Jackson county having been so named at my grandfather Fristoe's instance. Mother was descended from the Sullivans, Ladens and Percivals of South Carolina, the Taylors of Virginia and the Fristoes of Tennessee, and my grandfather Fristoe was a grand nephew of Chief Justice John Marshall of Virginia.

Naturally we were Southerners in sympathy and in fact. My father owned slaves and his children were reared in ease, though the border did not then abound in what would now be called luxury. The railroads had not reached Jackson county, and wild game was plentiful on my father's farm on Big Creek near Lee's Summit. I cannot remember when I did not know how to shoot. I hunted wild geese when I could not have dragged a pair of them home unaided. But this garden spot was destined to be a bloody battle ground when the nation divided.

There had been scrimmages back and forth over the Kansas line since 1855. I was only a boy, born January 15, 1844. My brother James was born January 15, 1848, John in 1851, and Robert in December, 1853. My eldest brother, Richard, died in 1860. This was before the conflicts and troubles centered on our home that planted a bitterness in my young heart which cried out for revenge and this feeling was only accentuated by the cruelties of war which followed. I refer in particular to the shameful and cowardly murder of my father for money which he was known to have in his possession, and the cruel treatment of my mother at the hands of the Missouri Militia. My father was in the employ of the United States government and had the mail contract for five hundred miles. While in Washington attending to some business regarding this matter, a raid was made by the Kansas Jayhawkers upon the livery stable and stage line for several miles out into the country, the robbers also looting his store and destroying his property generally. When my father returned from Washington and learned of these outrages he went to Kansas City, Mo., headquarters of the State Militia, to see if anything could be done. He had started back to Harrisonville in a buggy, but was waylaid one mile south of Westport, a suburb of Kansas City, and brutally murdered; falling out of his buggy into the road with three mortal bullet wounds. His horse was tied to a tree and his body left lying where it fell. Mrs. Washington Wells and her son, Samuel, on the road home from Kansas City to Lee's Summit, recognized the body as that of my father. Mrs. Wells stayed to guard the remains while her son carried the news of the murder to Col. Peabody of the Federal command, who was then in camp at Kansas City. An incident in connection with the murder of my father was the meeting of two of my cousins, on my mother's side, Charity Kerr and Nannie Harris (afterwards Mrs. McCorkle) with first my father and then a short distance on with Capt. Walley and his gang of the Missouri Militia, whose hands are stained with the blood of my father.

Walley afterwards caused the arrest of my cousins fearing that they had recognized him and his men. These young women were thrown into an old rickety, two-story house, located between 14th and 15th streets on Grand avenue, Kansas City, Mo. Twenty-five other women were also prisoners there at that time, including three of my own sisters. The down-stairs was used as a grocery store. After six months of living death in this trap, the house was secretly undermined and fell with the prisoners, only five of whom escaped injury or death. It was noted that the groceryman had moved his stock of groceries from the building in time to save it from ruin, showing that the wrecking of the house was planned in cold blood, with the murder of my sisters and cousins and the other unfortunate women in mind. All of my relatives, however, were saved from death except Charity Kerr, who was helpless in bed with the fever and she went down with the wreck and her body, frightfully mangled, was afterwards taken from the ruins. Mrs. McCorkle jumped from the window of the house and escaped. This cousin was the daughter of Reuben N. Harris, who was revenue collector for many years. A Virginian by birth, and a school teacher for many years in various parts of Missouri, he was well known throughout the state as an active sympathizer with the South. His home was friendly to every Confederate soldier and scout in the West. Information, newspapers, and the like, left there, were certain to be kept for the right hands.

In September 1863, soldiers ransacked the Harris home, stole everything they considered valuable, and burned the house. A daughter, Kate, who was asleep upstairs, was rescued from the flames by her sister. As the raiders left, one of them shouted:

"Now, old lady, call on your protectors. Why don't you call on Cole Younger now?"

Among the women who lost their lives was Miss Josephine Anderson, whose cruel death simply blighted her brother's life and so filled him with determination to revenge that he afterward became the most desperate of desperate men. "Quantrill sometimes spares, but Anderson never," became a tradition of the Kansas line.* Before he died in a skirmish with Northern troops in 1864, he had tied fifty-three knots in a silken cord which he carried in his buckskin pouch.

Every knot represented a human life.

Anderson was then ripe for the raid on Lawrence.

All this was cruelty, indeed, and enough to harden and embitter the softest of hearts, but it was mild compared with the continuous suffering and torture imposed upon my mother during the years from 1862 to 1870.

After the murder of my father she was so annoyed at her home in Harrisonville that she sought peace at her country residence eight and a half miles north of town. But she failed to find the comfort she sought, for annoyances continued in a more aggravated form. She had with her only the youngest children and was obliged to rely wholly for protection upon "Suse," the only remaining servant left to the family, who proved her worth many times over and in every emergency was loyalty and devotion itself. Nothing could have proved her faithfulness more effectually than an incident connected with one of my stolen visits home. I went home one night to get medicine for the boys wounded in the battle of Lone Jack whom I was nursing in the woods some miles away. As I sat talking with my mother two of my brothers watched at the windows. There was soon the dreaded cry, "the

* Cole Younger used the spelling "Quantrell"; this edition uses the more accepted "Quantrill."

militia are surrounding the house," and in the excitement which followed, "Suse" dashed open the door to find a score of bayonets in her face. She threw up her hands and pushed aside the guns. Her frantic screams, when they demanded that she deliver me up to them, caused a momentary confusion which enabled me to gain her side and together we made for the gate, where I took for the woods amid a shower of lead, none of the bullets even so much as skinning me, although from the house to the gate I was in the full glare of the light.

Two months after this incident the same persecutors again entered our home in the dead of the night, and, at the point of a pistol, tried to force my mother to set fire to her own home. She begged to be allowed to wait until morning, so that she and her children and "Suse" would not be turned out in the snow, then some two or three feet deep, in the darkness, with the nearest neighbor many miles away. This they agreed to do on condition that she put the torch to her house at daybreak. They were there bright and early to see that she carried out her agreement, so, leaving her burning walls behind her, she and the four youngest children and "Suse" began their eight mile trudge through the snow to Harrisonville.

I have always felt that the exposure to which she was subjected on this cruel journey, too hard even for a man to take, was the direct cause of her death. From Harrisonville she went to Waverly, where she was hounded continually. One of the conditions upon which her life was spared was that she would report at Lexington weekly. It was during one of her absences there that our enemies went to the house where she had left her family and demanded that they turn over the $2,200 which had been overlooked when my father was murdered. She had taken the precaution to conceal it upon the person of "Suse," and although they actually hung this faithful servant to a tree in the yard in their determination to force her to divulge the hiding place of the money, she never even hinted that the money at that very moment was secreted in her garments. She was left for dead, and except for the timely arrival of a friend, who cut her down and restored her to her senses, she would in a few moments have been as dead as her would-be-murderers hoped.

———

One of the numerous books purporting to be a history of my life states with the utmost soberness that, as a boy, I was cruel to dumb animals and to my schoolmates, and, as for my teachers, to them I was a continual trouble and annoyance. A hundred of my friends and schoolmates will bear me out in the statement that, far from being cruel to either dumb animals or human beings, I was always regarded as kind and considerate to both.

One of my old school-teachers, whom I have never seen since the spring or summer of 1862, is Stephen B. Elkins, senator from West Virginia.

July 4, 1898, Senator Elkins wrote: "I knew Cole Younger when we were boys and also his parents. They were good people and among the pioneers on the western border of Missouri. The Younger brothers maintained a good reputation in the community where they lived and were well esteemed, as were their parents, for their good conduct and character. In the spring or summer of 1862 I was taken prisoner by Quantrell's men and brought into his camp by the pickets who had me in charge. On reaching the camp the first person I saw whom I knew was Cole Younger. When I was taken prisoner, I expected to be shot without ceremony. As soon as I saw Cole Younger I felt a sense of relief because I had known him and his parents long and favorably, and as soon as I got a chance I told him frankly what I feared and that I hoped he would manage to take care of me and save me from being killed. He assured me he would do all he could to protect me. Cole Younger told Quantrell that my father and brother were in the rebel army and were good fighters, and that I had stayed at home to take care of my mother; that I was a good fellow and a non-combatant. This occurred just before I entered the Union army, and it was generally known, and I am sure Cole knew, that I was strongly for the Union and about to enter the army. Cole Younger told me what to do to make good my escape and I feel that I owe my life to his kindness."

Another old school-teacher is Capt. Steve Ragan, who still lives in Kansas City, Mo., and will bear testimony to the fact that I was neither cruel nor unmanageable.

2

The Dark and Bloody Ground

Many causes united in embittering the people on both sides of the border between Missouri and Kansas.

Those Missourians who were for slavery wanted Kansas admitted as a slave state, and sought to accomplish it by the most strenuous efforts. Abolitionists on the other hand determined that Kansas should be free and one of the plans for inviting immigration from the Eastern Northern states where slavery was in disrepute, was the organization of an Immigrant Aid Society, in which many of the leading men were interested. Neither the earnestness of their purpose nor the enthusiasm of their fight for liberty is for me to question now.

But many of those who came to Kansas under the auspices of this society were undesirable neighbors, looked at from any standpoint. Their ideas on property rights were very hazy, in many cases. Some of them were let out of Eastern prisons to live down a "past" in a new country. They looked upon a slave owner as legitimate prey, and later when lines became more closely drawn a secessionist was fit game, whether he had owned slaves or not.

These new neighbors ran off with the horses and negroes of

Missouri people without compunctions of conscience and some Missourians grew to have similarly lax notions about the property rights of Kansans. These raiders on both sides, if interfered with, would kill, and ultimately they developed into what was known during the war as "Freebooters," who, when they found a stable of horses or anything easily transportable, would take it whether the owner be abolitionist or secessionist in sympathy.

It was a robbery and murder by one of these bands of Kansas Jayhawkers, that gave to the Civil war Quantrill, the Chief of the Guerrillas.

A boy of 20, William Clarke Quantrill, had joined his brother in Kansas in 1855 and they were on their way to California overland when a band of Jayhawkers in command of Capt. Pickens, as was afterwards learned, raided their camp near the Cottonwood river; killed the older boy, left the younger one for dead, and carried off their valuables.

But under the care of friendly Indians, Charles Quantrill lived.

Changing his name to Charley Hart, he sought the Jayhawkers, joined Pickens' company, and confided in no one.

Quantrill and three others were sent out to meet an "underground railroad" train of negroes from Missouri. One of the party did not come back.

Between October, 1857, and March, 1858, Pickens' company lost 13 men. Promotion was rapid. Charley "Hart" was made a lieutenant.

No one had recognized in him the boy who had been left for dead two summers before, else Capt. Pickens had been more careful in his confidences. One night he told the young lieutenant the story of a raid on an emigrant camp on the Cottonwood river; how the dead man had been left no shroud; the wounded one no blanket; how the mules were sold and the proceeds gambled for.

But Lieut. "Hart's" mask revealed nothing.

Three days later Pickens and two of his friends were found dead on Bull Creek.

Col. Jim Lane's orderly boasted of the Cottonwood affair in his cups at a banquet one night.

The orderly was found dead soon after.

Quantrill told a friend that of the 32 who were concerned in the killing of his brother, only two remained alive, and they had moved to California.

The fight at Carthage in July 1861, found Quantrill in Capt. Stewart's company of cavalry. I was there as a private in the state guard, fighting under Price. Then came Gen. Lyon's fatal charge at Wilson's creek, and Gen. Price's march on Lexington to dislodge Col. Mulligan and his command.

Here Quantrill came into the public eye for the first time. His red shirt stood out in the first rank in every advance; he was one of the last when the men fell back.

After Lexington, Quantrill went with the command as far as the Osage river, and then, with the consent of his officers, came up the Kansas line again to settle some old scores with the Jayhawkers.

3

Driven from Home

I was only seventeen when Col. Mockbee gave a dancing party for his daughter at his home in Harrisonville which was to terminate seriously for some of us who were there.

The colonel was a Southerner, and his daughter had the Southern spirit, too. Probably this was the reason that inspired the young Missouri militiamen who were stationed at Harrisonville to intrude on the colonel's party. Among them was

Captain Irvin Walley, who, even though a married man, was par-
ticularly obnoxious in forcing his attentions on the young
women. My sister refused to dance with him, and he picked a
quarrel with me.

"Where is Quantrill?" he asked me, with a sneer.

"I don't know," I answered.

"You are a liar," he continued, and as he went down in a
heap on the floor, he drew his pistol, but friends came between
us, and at their solicitation I went home and informed my father
of what had taken place. He told me to go down to the farm in
Jackson county, and to keep away from the conflict that Walley
was evidently determined to force. Next morning I started. That
night Walley and a band of his scouts came to my father's house
and demanded that he surrender me, on the ground that I was
a spy, and in communication with Quantrill. Father denounced
it as a lie.

Though a slave-owner, father had never been in sympathy
with secession, believing, as it turned out, that it meant the
death of slavery. He was for the Union, in spite of his natural in-
clinations to sympathy with the South.

A demand that I surrender was conveyed to my father by Col.
Neugent, who was in charge of the militia at Harrisonville, again
charging that I was a spy. I never doubted that his action was due
to the enmity of Walley. My parents wanted me to go away to
school. I would have liked to have stayed and fought it out, and
although I consented to go away, it was too late, and I was left no
choice as to fighting it out. Watch was being kept for me at every
railroad station, and the only school I could reach was the school
of war close at home.

Armed with a shot-gun and revolver, I went out into the night
and was a wanderer.

Instant death to all persons bearing arms in Missouri was the
edict that went forth Aug. 30 of that year from Gen. John C. Fremont's headquarters at St. Louis, and he declared that all slaves

belonging to persons in arms against the United States were free. President Lincoln promptly overruled this, but it had added to the bitterness in Missouri where many men who owned slaves were as yet opposed to secession.

It was "hide and run for it" with me after that. That winter my brother-in-law, John Jarrette, and myself, joined Capt. Quantrill's company. Jarrette was orderly sergeant. He never knew fear, and the forty that then made up the company were as brave men as ever drew breath.

We were not long quiet. Burris had a detachment raiding in the neighborhood of Independence. We struck their camp at sunset. We were thirty-two; they eighty-four; but we were sure shots and one volley broke their ranks in utter confusion. Five fell at the first fire, and seven more died in the chase, the others regaining Independence, where the presence of the rest of the regiment saved them. That day my persistent pistol practice showed its worth when one of the militiamen fell, 71 yards away, actual measure. That was Nov. 10, 1861.

All that winter Independence was the scene of a bloody warfare. One day early in February Capt. Quantrill and David Pool, Bill Gregg and George Shepherd, George Todd and myself, charged in pairs down three of the streets to the court house, other members of the company coming through other streets. We had eleven hurt, but we got away with ammunition and other supplies that were badly needed. Seven militiamen died that day.

Another charge, at daybreak of Feb. 21, resulted badly. Instead of the one company we expected to find, there were four. Although we killed seventeen, we lost one, young George, who fell so close to the guns of the foe that we had considerable difficulty in getting him away for burial. Then we disbanded for a time. Capt. Quantrill believed that it was harder to trail one man than a company, and every little while the company would break up, to rally again at a moment's notice.

4

The Trap That Failed

In March Quantrill planned to attack Independence. We met at David George's and went from there toward Independence as far as Little Blue church, where Allen Parmer, who afterward married Susie James, the sister of Frank and Jesse, told the captain that instead of there being 300 Jayhawkers in Independence, there were 600. The odds were too strong, and we swung around to the southwest.

Thirteen soldiers who guarded the bridge at the Big Blue found their number unlucky. The bridge was burned and we dined that day at the home of Alex. Majors, of Russell, Majors & Waddell, the freighters, and rested for the night at Maj. Tate's house, near New Santa Fe, where there was fighting for sure before morning.

A militia command, 300 strong, came out to capture us, but they did not risk an attack until nearly midnight.

Capt. Quantrill, John Jarrette, and I were sleeping together when the alarm was given, the sentry's challenge, "Who are you?" followed by a pistol shot.

We were up on the instant.

So stealthy had been their approach that they had cut the sentry off from us before alarming him, and he fled into the timber in a shower of lead.

There was a heavy knock on the outer door, and a deep voice shouted: "Make a light."

Quantrill, listening within, fired through the panel. The visitor fell.

While we barricaded the windows with bedding, the captain polled his men. "Boys," he said, "we're in a tight place. We can't stay here and I do not mean to surrender. All who want to follow me out can say so; all who prefer to give up without a rush can also say so. I will do the best I can for them."

Four voted to surrender, and went out to the besieging party, leaving seventeen.

Quantrill, James Little, Hoy, Stephen Shores and myself held the upper story, Jarrette, George Shepherd, Toler and others the lower.

Anxious to see who their prisoners were, the militiamen exposed themselves imprudently, and it cost them six.

Would they permit Major Tate's family to escape? Yes. They were only too glad, for with the family out, the ell, which was not commanded by our fire, offered a tempting mark for the incendiary.

Hardly had the Tates left than the flames began to climb the ell.

There was another parley. Could we have twenty minutes? Ten? Five?

Back came the answer:

"You have one minute. If at its expiration you have not surrendered, not a single man among you shall escape alive."

"Thank you," said I; "catching comes before hanging."

"Count six then and be d—d to you!" shouted back George Shepherd, who was doing the dickering, and Quantrill said quietly, "Shotguns to the front."

There were six of these, and behind them came those with revolvers only. Then Quantrill opened the door and leaped out. Close behind him were Jarrette, Shepherd, Toler, Little, Hoy and myself, and behind us the revolvers.

In less time than it takes to tell it, the rush was over. We had lost five, Hoy being knocked down with a musket and taken prisoner, while they had eighteen killed and twenty-nine wounded.

We did not stop till we got to the timber, but there was really no pursuit. The audacity of the thing had given the troops a taste of something new.

They kept Hoy at Leavenworth for several months and then hanged him. This was the inevitable end of a "guerrilla" when taken prisoner.

5

Vengeance Indeed

Among the Jackson county folks who insisted on their right to shelter their friends was an old man named Blythe.

Col. Peabody at Independence had sent out a scouting party to find me or any one else of the company they could "beat up." Blythe was not at home when they came but his son, aged twelve, was. They took him to the barn and tried to find out where we were, but the little fellow baffled them until he thought he saw a chance to break through the guard, and started for the house.

He reached it safely, seized a pistol, and made for the woods followed by a hail of bullets. They dropped him in his tracks, but, game to the last, he rolled over as he fell, shot one of his pursuers dead, mortally wounded a second, and badly hurt a third.

They put seventeen bullets in him before he could shoot a fourth time.

A negro servant who had witnessed the seizure of his young master, had fled for the timber, and came upon a party of a dozen of us, including Quantrill and myself. As he quickly told us the story, we made our plans, and ambushed at the "Blue Cut," a deep pass on the road the soldiers must take back to Independence. The banks are about thirty feet high, and the cut about fifty yards wide.

Not a shot was to be fired until the entire command was in the cut.

Thirty-eight had started to "round up" Cole Younger that morning; seventeen of them lay dead in the cut that night and the rest of them had a lively chase into Independence.

To this day old residents know the Blue Cut as "the slaughter-pen."

Early in May, 1862, Quantrill's men were disbanded for a month. Horses were needed, and ammunition. There were plenty of horses in Missouri, but the ammunition presented more of a problem.

Capt. Quantrill, George Todd and myself, attired as Union officers, went to Hamilton, a small town on the Hannibal and St. Joseph Railroad, undetected by the company of the Seventh United States Cavalry in camp there, although we put up at the principal hotel. Todd passed as a major in the Sixth Missouri Cavalry, Quantrill a major in the Ninth, and I a captain in an Illinois regiment. At Hannibal there was a regiment of Federal soldiers. The commander talked very freely with us about Quantrill, Todd, Haller, Younger, Blunt, Pool and other guerrillas of whom he had heard.

While in Hannibal we bought 50,000 revolver caps and such other ammunition as we needed. From there we went to St. Joseph, which was under command of Col. Harrison B. Branch.

"Too many majors traveling together are like too many roses in a bouquet," suggested Todd. "The other flowers have no show."

He reduced himself to captain and I to lieutenant.

Our disguise was undiscovered. Col. Branch entertained us at his headquarters most hospitably.

"I hope you may kill a guerrilla with every bullet I have sold you," said one merchant to me. "I think if ever there was a set of devils let loose, it is Quantrill, Todd, Cole Younger and Dave Pool."

From St. Joseph we went to Kansas City in a hack, sending Todd into Jackson county with the ammunition. When within three miles of Kansas City the hack was halted by a picket on outpost duty, and while the driver argued with the guard, Quantrill and I slipped out on the other side of the hack and made our way to William Bledsoe's farm, where we were in friendly hands.

6

In the Enemy's Lines

Col. Buell, whose garrison of 600 held Independence, had ordered that every male citizen of Jackson county between 18 and 45 years of age should fight against the South.

Col. Upton Hays, who was in Jackson county in July and August, 1862, recruiting a regiment for the Confederate army, decided that it was the time to strike a decisive blow for the dislodging of Buell. In reconnoitering the vicinity he took with him Dick Yager, Boone Muir and myself, all of whom had seen service with Capt. Quantrill.

It was finally decided to make the attack August 11th. Colonel Hays wanted accurate information about the state of things inside town.

"Leave that to me," said I.

Three days remained before the battle.

Next morning there rode up to the picket line at Independence an old apple-woman, whose gray hair and much of her face was nearly hidden by an old-fashioned and faded sun-bonnet. Spectacles half hid her eyes and a basket on her arm was laden with beets, beans and apples.

The left rein was leather but a rope replaced the right.

"Good morning, grandmother," bantered the first picket. "Does the rebel crop need any rain out in your country?"

The sergeant at the reserve post seized her bridle, and looking up said:

"Were you younger and prettier, I might kiss you."

"Were I younger and prettier, I might box your ears for your impudence."

"Oh, ho! You old she-wolf, what claws you have for scratching!" he retorted, and reached for her hand.

The quick move she made started the horse suddenly, or he might have been surprised to feel that hand.

But the horse was better than apple-women usually ride, and that aroused some suspicion at Col. Buell's headquarters, so that the ride out was interrupted by a mounted picket who galloped alongside and again her bridle was seized.

The sergeant and eight men of the guard were perhaps thirty paces back.

"What will you have?" asked the apple-woman. "I am but a poor lone woman going peaceably to my home."

"Didn't you hear the sergeant call for you, d—n you?" answered the sentinel.

A spurred boot under the ragged skirt pierced the horse's flank; the hand that came from the apple basket fired the cocked pistol almost before the sentry knew it, and the picket fell dead.

The reserve stood as if stupefied.

That night I gave Quantrill, for Col. Hays, a plan showing the condition of affairs in Independence.

The morning of the 11th the attack was made and Col. Buell, his force shot to pieces, surrendered.

The apple-woman's expedition had been a success.

7

Lone Jack

It was in August, 1862, nearly a year after the party at Col. Mockbee's, that I was formally enrolled in the army of the Confederate States of America by Col. Gideon W. Thompson. I was eighteen, and for some little time had been assisting Col. Hays in recruiting a regiment around my old home.

It was within a day or two after the surrender of Buell at Independence that I was elected as first lieutenant in Capt. Jarrette's company in Col. Upton B. Hays' regiment, which was a part of the brigade of Gen. Joseph O. Shelby.

We took the oath, perhaps 300 of us, down on Luther Mason's farm, a few miles from where I now write, where Col. Hays had encamped after Independence.

Millions of boys and men have read with rising hair the terrible "black oath" which was supposed to have been taken by these brave fighters, but of which they never heard, nor I, until I read it in books published long after the war.

When Col. Hays camped on the Cowherd, White, Howard and Younger farms, Quantrill had been left to guard the approaches to Kansas City, and to prevent the escape to that point of news from the scattered Confederate commands which were recruiting in western Missouri. At the same time he was obtaining from the Chicago and St. Louis papers and other sources, information about the northern armies, which was conveyed by couriers to Confederate officers in the south, and he kept concealed along the Missouri river skiffs and ferry boats to enable the Confederate officers, recruiting north of the river, to have free access to the south.

The night that I was enlisted, I was sent by Col. Hays to meet Cols. Cockrell, Coffee, Tracy, Jackman and Hunter, who, with the remnants of regiments that had been shattered in various battles through the south, were headed toward Col. Hays' command.

It was Col. Hays' plan for them to join him the fifteenth, and after a day's rest, the entire command would attack Kansas City, and, among other advantages resulting from victory there, secure possession of Weller's steam ferry.

Boone Muir and myself met Coffee and the rest below Rose Hill, on Grand river. Col. Cockrell, whose home was in Johnson county, had gone by a different route, hoping to secure new recruits among his neighbors, and, as senior colonel, had directed the rest of the command to encamp the next evening at Lone Jack, a little village in the southeastern portion of Jackson county, so called from a solitary big black jack tree that rose from an open field nearly a mile from any other timber.

At noon of Aug. 15, Muir and I had been in the saddle twenty-four to thirty hours, and I threw myself on the blue grass to sleep.

Col. Hays, however, was still anxious to have the other command join him, he having plenty of forage, and being well equipped with ammunition as the result of the capture of Independence a few days before. Accordingly I was shortly awakened to accompany him to Lone Jack, where he would personally make known the situation to the other colonels.

Meantime, however, Major Emory L. Foster, in command at Lexington, had hurried out to find Quantrill, if possible, and avenge Independence. Foster had nearly 1,000 cavalrymen, and two pieces of Rabb's Indiana battery that had already made for itself a name for hard fighting. He did not dream of the presence of Cockrell and his command until he stumbled upon them in Lone Jack.

At nightfall, the Indiana battery opened on Lone Jack, and the Confederate commands were cut in two, Coffee retreating to the south, while Cockrell withdrew to the west, and when Col. Hays and I arrived, had his men drawn up in line of battle, while the officers were holding a council in his quarters.

"Come in, Colonel Hays," exclaimed Col. Cockrell. "We just sent a runner out to look you up. We want to attack Foster and beat him in the morning. He will just be a nice breakfast spell."

Col. Hays sent me back to bring up his command, but on second thought said:

"No, Lieutenant, I'll go, too."

On the way back he asked me what I thought about Foster being a "breakfast spell."

"I think he'll be rather tough meat for breakfast," I replied. "He might be all right for dinner."

But Cockrell and Foster were neighbors in Johnson county, and Cockrell did not have as good an idea of Foster's fighting qualities that night as he did twenty-four hours later.

The fight started at daybreak, hit or miss, an accidental gunshot giving Foster's men the alarm. For five hours it waged, most of the time across the village street, not more than sixty feet wide, and during those five hours every recruit there felt the force of Gen. Sherman's characterization—"War is hell."

Jackman, with a party of thirty seasoned men, charged the Indiana guns, and captured them, but Major Foster led a gallant charge against the invaders, and recaptured the pieces. We were out of ammunition, and were helpless, had the fight been pressed.

Riding to the still house where we had left the wagon munitions we had taken a few days before at Independence, I obtained a fresh supply and started for the action on the gallop.

Of that mad ride into the camp I remember little except that

I had my horse going at full tilt before I came into the line of fire. Although the enemy was within 150 yards, I was not wounded. They did mark my clothes in one or two places, however.

Major Foster, in a letter to Judge George M. Bennett of Minneapolis, said:

"During the progress of the fight my attention was called to a young Confederate riding in front of the Confederate line, distributing ammunition to the men from what seemed to be a 'splint basket.' He rode along under a most galling fire from our side the entire length of the Confederate lines, and when he had at last disappeared, our boys recognized his gallantry in ringing cheers. I was told by some of our men from the western border of the state that they recognized the daring young rider as Cole Younger. About 9:30 A.M., I was shot down. The wounded of both forces were gathered up and were placed in houses. My brother and I, both supposed to be mortally wounded, were in the same bed. About an hour after the Confederates left the field, the ranking officer who took command when I became unconscious, gathered his men together and returned to Lexington. Soon after the Confederates returned. The first man who entered my room was a guerrilla, followed by a dozen or more men who seemed to obey him. He was personally known to me and had been my enemy from before the war. He said he and his men had just shot a lieutenant of a Cass county company whom they found wounded and that he would shoot me and my brother. While he was standing over us, threatening us with his drawn pistol, the young man I had seen distributing ammunition along in front of the Confederate line rushed into the room from the west door and seizing the fellow, thrust him out of the room. Several Confederates followed the young Confederate into the room, and I heard them call him Cole Younger. He (Younger) sent for Col. Cockrell (in command of the Confederate forces) and stated the case to him. He also called the young man Cole Younger and directed him to guard the house, which he did. My brother had with him about

$300, and I had about $700. This money and our revolvers were, with the knowledge and approval of Cole Younger, placed in safe hands, and were finally delivered to my mother in Warrensburg, Mo. Cole Younger was then certainly a high type of manhood, and every inch a soldier, who risked his own life to protect that of wounded and disabled enemies. I believe he still retains those qualities and would prove himself as good a citizen as we have among us if set free, and would fight for the Stars and Stripes as fearlessly as he did for the Southern flag. I have never seen him since the battle of Lone Jack. I know much of the conditions and circumstances under which the Youngers were placed after the war, and knowing this, I have great sympathy for them. Many men, now prominent and useful citizens of Missouri, were, like the Youngers, unable to return to their homes until some fortunate accident threw them with men they had known before the war, who had influence enough to make easy their return to peace and usefulness. If this had occurred to the Youngers, they would have had good homes in Missouri."

It is to Major Foster's surprise of the command at Lone Jack that Kansas City owes its escape from being the scene of a hard battle August 17, 1862.

Quantrill was not in the fight at Lone Jack at all, but Jarrette and Gregg did come up with some of Quantrill's men just at the end and were in the chase back toward Lexington.

In proportion to the number of men engaged, Lone Jack was one of the hardest fights of the war. That night there were 136 dead and 550 wounded on the battlefield.

8

A Foul Crime

With two big farms in Jackson county, besides money-making stores and a livery stable at Harrisonville, my father at the outbreak of the war was wealthy beyond the average of the people in northwestern Missouri. As a mail contractor, his stables were filled with good horses, and his property was easily worth $100,000, which was much more in those days, in the public esteem, than it is now.

This, perhaps, as much as Walley's enmity for me, made him the target for the freebooters who infested the Kansas line. In one of Jennison's first raids, the Younger stable at Harrisonville was raided and $20,000 worth of horses and vehicles taken. The experiment became a habit with the Jayhawkers, and such visits were frequent until the following fall, when the worst of all the indignities heaped upon my family was to be charged against them—the murder of my father.

When the body was discovered, it was taken in charge by Capt. Peabody, who was in command of the militia forces in Kansas City, and when he found $2,000, which father had taken the precaution to conceal in a belt which he wore about him, it was sent home to our family.

It has been charged that my father tried to draw his pistol on a party of soldiers, who suspected me of the murder of one of their comrades and wanted to know my whereabouts. This is false. My father never carried a pistol, to my knowledge, and I have never had any doubt that the band that killed him was led by that same Capt. Walley. Indeed he was suspected at the time, accused of murder, and placed under arrest, but his comrades furnished an alibi, to the satisfaction of the court, and he was released.

He is dead now, and probably he rests more comfortably than he ever did after that night in '62, for whether he had a conscience or not, he knew that Missouri people had memories, and good ones, too.

But the freebooters were not through.

My sisters were taken prisoners, as were the girls of other families whose sons had gone to join the Confederate army, their captors hoping by this means to frighten the Southern boys into surrender.

After my mother's home was burned, she took her children and went to Lafayette county. Militiamen followed her, shot at Jim, the oldest of the boys at home, fourteen, and drove him into the brush. Small wonder that he followed his brother as a soldier when he became old enough in 1864!

Despairing of peace south of the Missouri, mother crossed into Clay county, remaining until the War between the States had ended. But not so the war on her. A mob, among whom she recognized some of the men who were pretty definitely known to have murdered my father, broke in on her after she had returned to Jackson county, searched the house for Jim and me, hung John, aged fourteen, to a beam and told him to say his prayers, for he had but a little time to live unless he told where his older brothers were. He defied them and was strung up four times. The fourth time the rope cut deep into the flesh. The boy was unconscious. Brutally hacking his body with knives, they left him for dead. That was early in 1870.

June 2 of that year, before John had recovered from his injuries, mother died.

9

How Elkins Escaped

It was along about the first week in October, 1862, that I stopped with a dozen men at the home of Judge Hamilton, on Big Creek, in Cass county. We spent the afternoon there, and just before leaving John Hays, of my command, dashed up with the news that Quantrill was camped only two miles west. He also gave the more important information to me, that some of Captain Parker's men had arrested Steve Elkins on the charge of being a Union spy, and were taking him to Quantrill's camp to hang him.

I lost no time in saddling up, and followed by my little detachment, rode hastily away to Quantrill's camp, for red tape occupied little space in those days, and quick action was necessary if anything was to be done.

I knew Quantrill and his men well and was also aware that there were several Confederate officers in the camp. The moment we reached our destination, I went at once to Captain Charles Harrison, one of the officers, and my warm personal friend, and told him openly of my friendship and esteem for Elkins. He promised to lend me all his aid and influence, and I started out to see Quantrill, after first telling my men to keep their horses saddled, ready for a rescue and retreat in case I failed of a peaceable deliverance.

Quantrill received me courteously and kindly, as he always did, and after a little desultory chat, I carelessly remarked, "I am surprised to find that you have my old friend and teacher, Steve Elkins, in camp as a prisoner."

"What! Do you know him?" asked Quantrill in astonishment.

I told him that I did, and that he was my school teacher when the war broke out, also that some half a hundred other pupils of Elkins were now fighting in the Southern army.

"We all care for him very deeply," I told Quantrill, and then asked what charges were preferred against him. He explained that Elkins had not been arrested on his orders, but by some of Parker's men, who were in vicious humor because of their leader's recent death. They had told Quantrill that Elkins had joined the Union forces at Kansas City, and was now in Cass county as a spy.

I jumped to my feet, and said that the men that made the charges lied, and that I stood ready to ram the lie down their throats with a pistol point. Quantrill laughed, and chided me about letting my hot blood get the better of cold judgment. I insisted, however, and told him further that Elkins' father and brother were Southern soldiers, and that Steve was a non-combatant, staying at home to care for his mother, but that I was in no sense a non-combatant, and would stand as his champion in any fight.

Quantrill finally looked at his watch, and then remarked: "I will be on the move in fifteen minutes. I will release Elkins, since you seem so excited about it, and will leave him in your hands. Be careful, for Parker's men are rather bitter against him."

Happy at heart, I dashed away to see Elkins, with whom I had only passed a few words and a hand-shake to cheer him up. He knew me, however, and realized that I would save him or die in the attempt, for from a boy it was my reputation that I never deserted a friend.

When I joined him again, several of Parker's men were standing around in the crowd, and as I shook hands with Elkins and told him of his freedom, I added, "If any damned hound makes further false charges against you, it's me he's got to settle with, and that at the pistol point."

I made that talk as a sort of bluff, for a bluff is often as good as a fight if it's properly backed up. As Quantrill and his men rode away in the direction of Dave Daily's neighborhood, I told Elkins to hit out West until he came to the Kansas City and Harrisonville road, and then, under cover of night, he could go either way. I shook his hand goodbye, slapped him on the shoulder, and have never seen him since.

I followed Quantrill's men for half a mile, fearing that some stragglers might return to take a quiet shot at Elkins, and then stopped for something to eat, and fed our horses.

At the time that I defended Elkins before Quantrill, I knew that Steve's sympathies were with the North, and had heard that he had joined the Federal army. But it mattered nothing to me— he was my friend.

10

A Price on My Head

When Col. Hays went south in the fall to join Shelby, Capt. Jarrette went with as many of his company as were able to travel and the wounded were left with me in Jackson county.

Missouri militia recognized no red cross, and we were unable for that reason to shelter our men in farm-houses, but built dugouts in the hills, the roofs covered with earth for concealment.

All that winter we lay in the hollows of Jackson county, while the militia sought to locate the improvised hospitals.

It was a winter of battles too numerous to be told here, and it was a winter, too, that laid a price upon my head.

Capt. Quantrill and his men had raided Olathe and Shawneetown, and among the killed at Paola on the way out from Olathe was a man named Judy, whose father had formerly lived in Cass county, but had gone to Kansas as a refugee. Judy, the father, returned to Cass county after the war as the appointive sheriff.

It was a matter of common knowledge to the guerillas, at least that young Judy had been killed by Dick Maddox and Joe Hall, and that as a matter of fact at the time of the fight I was miles away at Austin, Mo. But Judy had secured my indictment in Kansas on the charge of killing his son, and threatened me with arrest by a posse so that from 1863 to 1903 I was never in Cass county except as a hunted man. Years afterward this killing of Judy turned up to shut me out of Missouri.

Frequent meetings with the militia were unavoidable during the winter and there was fight after fight. Clashes were almost daily, but few of them involved any large number of men.

George Todd and Albert Cunningham, who were also caring for squads of soldiers in our neighborhood, and I made an expedition early in the winter across the Kansas line near New Santa Fe, where our party of 30 met 62 militiamen. Todd led the charge. With a yell and a rush, every man with a revolver in each hand, they gave the militia a volley at a hundred yards, which was returned, but no men could stand in the face of a rush like that and the militia fell back. In their retreat they were reinforced by 150 more and returned to the attack, driving Todd and his comrades before them. With six men I was holding the rear in the timber when a detachment of 52 ran down upon us. It was a desperate fight, and every man in it was wounded more or less. John McDowell's horse was killed under him and he, wounded, called to me for help.

Packing him up behind me, we returned to our camp in safety.

This was the McDowell who less than three months later betrayed one of our camps to the militia in Independence and brought down upon us a midwinter raid.

Todd had his camp at Red Crenshaw's, Cunningham was on

the Little Blue, and mine was near Martin O. Jones' farm, eight miles south of Independence.

Todd's spirit of adventure, with my hope to avenge my father's murder, combined in a Christmas adventure which has been misrepresented by other writers.

Todd said he knew some of the band who had killed father were in Kansas City, and Christmas day six of us went in to look them up.

Leaving Zach Traber with our horses just beyond the outposts, the rest of us hunted them until it must have been nearly midnight. We were in a saloon on Main street. I had called for a cigar, and glancing around, saw that we had been recognized by a trooper who had been playing cards. He reached for his pistol, but he never pulled it.

I do not know how many were killed that night. They chased us well out of town and there was a fight at the picket post on the Independence road.

Col. Penick, in command at Independence, hearing of the Kansas City adventure, put a price of $1,000 on my head and other figures on those of my comrades.

It was to get this blood money that six weeks later, Feb. 9, the militia drove my mother out of her house and made her burn it before their eyes.

I was a hunted man.

11

Betrayed

The day after they burned my mother out of her home they made another trial for the $1,000 reward, and this time they had a better prospect of success, for they had with them the traitor, McDowell, whom I had carried out on my horse in the fight at New Santa Fe a few weeks before. McDowell said he wanted to go home to see his wife and assure her he was all right, but he did not go near her. Instead he hurried into Independence and that evening the militia came out, eighty strong, to take us prisoners. Even they did not trust McDowell, for he, closely guarded, was kept in front.

Forty of them had come within twenty yards of us on the south when my horse warned me, and I called out: "Is that you Todd?"

"Don't mind us; we're friends," came the answer, but I saw they were not, and the lieutenant in command fell at the first fire. The boys swarmed out of the dug-outs, and the fighting was hot. Retreat to the north was cut off by the other forty and they had us between them. We made for the west, firing as we went, and the soldiers fell right and left. I stayed by Joe Hardin till they dropped him in his tracks, and fought fifteen of the militia while Otho Hinton stopped to get his heavy boots off. Tom Talley, too, had one boot off and one foot stuck in the leg of the other. He could not run and he had no knife to cut the leather. I yanked his boot off and we took to our heels, the militia within 20 yards. Talley's pistol had filled with snow and he could not fire a shot. But we reached the timber and stood at bay. George Talley was shot dead at this last stand, but when the militia fell back, their dead and wounded numbered seventeen. Nathan Kerr, Geo. Wigginton, Bill Hulse and John McCorkle did well that day.

We were all in our socks, having taken off our overcoats, gloves and heavy boots to lighten our burdens, and the icy road promised to cut our feet to pieces, but we made our way to a rock bridge where a hog trail would hide our tracks, and when we left this trail, I made every one of the boys follow in my footprints, leaving but the one trail till we got to the cedar bluffs. For a stretch of three miles here, these bluffs were practically impassable to horsemen, but we climbed down them and found our way to the home of Mrs. Moore where we were safe again.

The soldiers took back to Independence a pair of gloves marked "Presented to Lieut. Coleman Younger by Miss M. E. Sanders" and they thought Cole Younger was dead for a time. Her brother, Charles Sanders, was one of my company.

Making our way out to Napoleon and Wellington we got new coats and gloves and also located some of the red sheepskin leggings worn by the Red-leg scouts, with which we made a trip over into what was known as "Hell's corner" on the Missouri, near Independence. Col. Penick's men, who had in many cases "collected" more horses than they really had use for, had left them with friends at various points. As we went in we spotted as many of these as we thought we could lead out, and took them out with us on our way back.

One of the horses I got on that trip was the meanest horse I ever rode and I named him "Jim Lane" in honor of one of the most efficient raiders that ever disgraced an army uniform. This horse a young woman was keeping for her sweetheart who had left it with her father for safety, as he feared it might be shot. As I mounted the nag, she suddenly grasped the bridle reins. The horse always, I found afterwards, had a trick of rearing up on his hind feet, when he was about to start off. Evidently the young woman was also ignorant of his little habit or else she would never have taken hold of his bridle in an effort to detain me. He was no respecter of persons, this horse of her sweetheart, and he rose high in the air with the young woman still clinging. He turned around and made almost a complete circuit before he came down and again allowed her to enjoy the security of having both feet upon the earth. She was a little frightened after having been lifted off her feet in this way and dangled in the air, and somewhat piqued, too, that I was about to ride away on her sweetheart's horse, and when I suggested that the horse was not as quiet as he might be and she had better not catch hold of his bridle any more, she called to me as a parting shot, "You horrid old red-leg, you are meaner than Quantrill or Todd or Cole Younger or any of his gang!"

The night we made our escape, they burned the homes of Grandmother Fristoe, and her neighbor, Mrs. Rucker, and gray heads suffered because younger ones had not been noosed.

12

Quantrill on War

After the Lone Jack fight, Capt. Quantrill had joined Gen. Shelby at Cane Hill, Arkansas, but shortly left his command to go to the Confederate capital at Richmond to ask to be commissioned as a colonel under the partisan ranger act and to be so recognized by the war department as to have any protection the Confederate States might be able to afford him. He knew the service was a furious one, but he believed that to succeed the South must fight desperately.

Secretary Cooper suggested that war had its amenities and refinements and that in the nineteenth century it was simply barbarism to talk of a black flag.

"Barbarism," rejoined Quantrill, according to Senator Louis T. Wigfall, of Texas, who was present at the interview, "barbarism, Mr. Secretary, means war and war means barbarism. You ask an impossible thing, Mr. Secretary. This secession or revolution, or whatever you call it, cannot conquer without violence. Your young Confederacy wants victory. Men must be killed."

"What would you do, Captain Quantrill, were yours the power and the opportunity?" inquired the secretary.

"Do, Mr. Secretary? I would wage such a war as to make surrender forever impossible. I would break up foreign enlistments by indiscriminate massacre. I would win the independence of my people or I would find them graves."

"What of our prisoners?"

"There would be no prisoners," exclaimed the fiery captain. "Do they take any prisoners from me? Surrounded, I do not surrender; hunted, I hunt my hunters; hated and made blacker than a dozen devils, I add to my hoofs the swiftness of a horse and to my horns the terrors of a savage following. Kansas should be laid waste at once. Meet the torch with the torch, pillage with pillage, slaughter with slaughter, subjugation with extermination. You have my ideas of war, Mr. Secretary, and I am sorry they do not accord with your own or with the ideas of the government you have the honor to represent so well."

Disappointed, Capt. Quantrill left without his commission. He had felt the truth of his fiery speech.

Our tenders of exchanges of prisoners had been scorned by the officers of the militia. There was a boy who was an exception to this rule, to whom I want to pay a tribute. He was a young lieutenant from Brown county and if my memory serves me right, his name also was Brown. We had taken him prisoner at Olathe.

At Leavenworth they had one of our boys named Hoy, who had been taken at the Tate house, and we paroled Brown, and sent him to Leavenworth to ask the exchange of Hoy.

Brown went, too, and was laughed at for his earnestness. Exchange was ridiculed. "You are free," they said to him, "why worry about exchanges?"

But Brown had given his word as a man and as a soldier and he came back to our camp and surrendered. He was told to return to the lines of his own army, and given safe conduct and money to provide for his immediate wants, but he vowed he would never fight again under his country's flag until he had been exchanged in accordance with his parole.

There was a cheer for that man when he left the camp, and anyone who had proposed shooting him would himself have been riddled.

13

The Palmyra Butchery

As long as Pete Donan was the editor of the Lexington Caucasian, that paper once each year published an account substantially in this wise:

"So long as God gives us life and the earth is cursed with the presence of McNeil we feel it to be our solemn duty to rehearse once every year the story of the most atrocious and horrible occurrence in the annals of barbarous warfare.

"On Friday, the 17th day of October, 1862, a deed was enacted at the fair grounds at Palmyra, Mo., which sent a thrill of horror through the civilized world.

"Ten brave and true and innocent men were taken from their prison, driven to the edge of the town, seated on their rough board coffins, for no crime of their own, and murdered like so many swine.

"Murdered!

"Butchered!!

"By the hell-spanned and hell-bound, trebly damned old blotch upon creation's face, John McNeil, until recently by the grace of bayonets, Tom Fletcher, and the devil, sheriff of St. Louis county.

"Murdered!

"Shot to death!!

"There was our poor, handsome, gallant boyhood friend Tom Sidener—

"As pure a soul as ever winged its flight from blood-stained sod to that God who will yet to all eternity damn the fiendish butcher, McNeil.

"Poor Tom!

"He was engaged to be married to a young lady in Monroe county.

"When he learned he was to be shot, he sent for his wedding suit, which had just been made, declaring that if he couldn't be married in it; he intended to die in it.

"Arrayed in his elegant black broad cloth, and his white silk vest, when he mounted his coarse plank coffin, in the wagon that was to bear him to his death he looked as if he was going to be married instead of shot.

"The very guards cried like children when they bade him goodbye.

"Raising his cap and bowing to the weeping women who lined the streets, he was driven from their sight forever!

"Half an hour afterward six musket balls had pierced his noble heart, and his white silk vest was torn and dyed with his martyr blood!

"There was poor old Willis Baker, his head whitened with the snows of more than seventy winters—

"Heroic old man!

"With his white hair streaming in the wind, he seated himself on his rude coffin and died without a shudder; refusing with his last breath to forgive his executioners, and swearing he would 'meet them and torment them in hell through all eternity.'

"There was that helpless, half-idiot boy from Lewis county, who allowed himself to be blindfolded; then hearing Sidener and the others refuse, slipped up one corner of the bandage, and seeing the rest with their eyes uncovered, removed the handkerchief from his own, died as innocent as a lamb.

"There were Humstead and Bixler, and Lake, and McPheeters.

"And there was that most wondrous martyr of them all—young Smith, of Knox county—who died for another man.

"Humphrey was the doomed man.

"His heart-broken wife, in widow's weeds, with her eight helpless little ones in deep mourning, that was only less black than the anguish they endured, or the heart of him to whom they appealed, rushed to the feet of McNeil, and in accents so piteous that a soul of adamant must have melted under it, besought him for the life of the husband and father.

"She was brutally repulsed.

"But Strachan, the monster of Shelby county, whom the angel a few months afterward smote with Herodian rottenness—Strachan, whose flesh literally fell from his living skeleton—Strachan, who has long been paying in the deepest, blackest, hottest hole in perdition the penalty of his forty-ply damnation-deserving crimes was provost marshal.

"He saw the frantic agony of the woman; called her into his office and told her he would save her husband if she would give him three hundred dollars and then submit—but oh! humanity shudders, sickens at the horrid proposal.

"The wretched, half-crazed, agonized wife, not knowing what she did—acceded to save her husband's life—and the next morning she was found lying insane and nearly dead, with her baby at her breast, near the public spring at Palmyra.

"And after all this, her husband was only released on condition that another should be shot in his place.

"Young Smith was selected.

"And then ensued a contest without a parallel in all the six thousand years of human history.

"Humphrey refused to let any man die in his stead, declaring he should feel himself a murderer if he did.

"Smith protested that he was only a poor orphan boy, and so far as he knew there was not a soul on earth to grieve for him; that

Humphrey had a large family entirely dependent upon him for daily bread, and it was his duty to live while he could.

"And Smith, the simple country lad, only seventeen years old, the Hero without a peer on all Fame's mighty scroll, took his seat on a rough box—and was shot!

"Will not God eternally damn his murderers?

"We might dwell for hours on the incidents connected with this most frightful butchery of ancient or modern ages.

"But why go on?

"The murder was done!

"The Confederate government talked of demanding the murderer McNeil.

"Then a 'memorial' was gotten up, and signed by two thousand Missourians, recommending the heaven-earth-and-hell-accursed old monster, on account of his Palmyra massacre, to special favor and he was promoted to a brigadier-generalship."

14

Lawrence

Disguised as a cattle trader, Lieutenant Fletcher Taylor, now a prominent and wealthy citizen of Joplin, Mo., spent a week at the Eldridge house in Lawrence, Kansas, from which place had gone out the Jayhawkers who in three months just previous had slain 200 men and boys, taken many women prisoners, and stolen no one knows how many horses.

At the house of Capt. Purdee on the Blackwater in Johnson county, 310 men answered August 16, 1863, to the summons of Capt. Quantrill to hear the report of Lieut. Taylor's reconnaissance.

The lieutenant's report was encouraging. The city itself was poorly garrisoned; the camp beyond was not formidable; the streets were wide.

"You have heard the report," said Quantrill when the lieutenant finished. "It is a long march; we march through soldiers; we attack soldiers; we must retreat through soldiers. What shall it be? Speak out. Anderson!"

"Lawrence or hell," relied Anderson, instantly. With fire flashing in his eyes as he recalled the recent wreck from which his sister had been taken in Kansas City, he added: "But with one proviso, that we kill every male thing."

"Todd?" called Quantrill.

"Lawrence, if I knew that not a man would get back alive."

"Gregg?"

This was Capt. William Gregg, who still lives in Kansas City, one of the bravest men that ever faced powder, and in action the coolest, probably, in the entire command.

"Lawrence," he relied. "It is the home of Jim Lane; the nurse of Jayhawkers."

"Jarrette?"

"Lawrence, by all means," my brother-in-law answered. "It is the head devil of the killing and burning in Jackson county. I vote to fight it and with fire burn it before we leave."

Shepherd, Dick Maddox, so on, Quantrill called the roll.

"Have you all voted?" shouted Quantrill.

There was no word.

"Then Lawrence it is; saddle up."

We reached Lawrence the morning of the 21st. Quantrill sent me to quiz an old farmer who was feeding his hogs as to whether there had been any material changes in Lawrence since Lieut. Taylor had been there. He thought there were 75 soldiers in Lawrence; there were really 200.

Four abreast, the column dashed into the town with the cry: "The camp first!"

It was a day of butchery. Bill Anderson claimed to have killed fourteen and the count was allowed. But it is not true that women were killed. One negro woman leaned out of a window and shouted:

"You —— of —— ."

She toppled out dead before it was seen she was a woman.

The death list that day is variously estimated at from 143 to 216 and the property loss by the firing of the town, the sacking of the bank, and the rest, at $1,500.000.

Maj. John N. Edwards, in his "Noted Guerrillas," says:

"Cole Younger saved at least a dozen lives this day. Indeed, he killed none save in open and manly battle. At one house he captured five citizens over whom he put a guard and at another three whom he defended and protected. The notorious Gen. James H. Lane, to get whom Quantrell would gladly have left and sacrificed all the balance of the victims, made his escape through a corn-field, hotly pursued but too splendidly mounted to be captured."

My second lieutenant, Lon Railey, and a detachment gave Jim Lane a hot chase that day but in vain.

When I joined Brother-in-law Jarrette's company, he said:

"Cole, your mother and your sister told me to take care of you."

That day it was reversed. Coming out of Lawrence his horse was shot under him. He took the saddle off and tried to put it on a mustang that one of the boys was leading. Some of the boys say he had $8,ooo in the saddle bags for the benefit of the widows and orphans of Missouri, but whether that is true or not I have no knowledge. While he was trying to saddle the mustang, he was nearly surrounded by the enemy. I dashed back and made him get up behind me. The saddle was left for the Kansas men.

One of the treasures that we did bring out of Lawrence that day, however, was Jim Lane's "black flag," with the inscription

"Presented to Gen. James H. Lane by the ladies of Leaven-worth."

That is the only black flag that I knew anything about in connection with the Lawrence raid.

Lawrence was followed by a feverish demand from the North for vengeance. Quantrill was to be hanged, drawn and quartered, his band annihilated; nothing was too terrible for his punishment.

Four days after the raid, Gen. Thomas Ewing at St. Louis issued his celebrated General Order No. 11. This required that all persons living in Jackson, Cass and Bates counties, except one township, or within one mile of a military post, should remove within fifteen days. Those establishing their loyalty were permitted to go within the lines of any military post, or to Kansas, but all others were to remove without the bounds of the military district. All grain and hay in the proscribed district was to be turned into the military post before Sept. 9, and any grain or hay not so turned in was to be destroyed.

It was the depopulation of western Missouri. Any citizen not within the limits of the military post after Sept. 9 was regarded as an outlaw.

Pursued by 6,000 soldiers, the Confederates in that vicinity must ultimately rejoin their army farther south, but they harassed their pursuers for weeks in little bands rarely exceeding ten.

The horrors of guerrilla warfare before the raid at Lawrence, were eclipsed after it. Scalping, for the first time, was resorted to.

Andy Blunt found Ab. Haller's body, so mutilated, in the woods near Texas Prairie on the eastern edge of Jackson county.

"We had something to learn yet," said Blunt to his companions, "and we have learned it. Scalp for scalp hereafter."

Among the brave fighters who were participants in the fight at Lawrence were Tom Maupin, Dick Yager, Payne Jones, Frank Shepherd, Harrison Trow, Dick Burns, Andy McGuire and Ben Broomfield.

15

Chasing Cotton Thieves

In the fall of 1863, in the absence of Capt. Jarrette, who had re-joined Shelby's command, I became, at 19, captain of the company. Joe Lea was first lieutenant and Lon Railey second lieutenant.

When Capt. Jarrette came north again, I again became lieutenant, but when Capts. Jarrette and Poole reported to Gen. Shelby on the Red river, they were sent into Louisiana, and I again became captain of the company, so reporting to Gen. Henry E. McCulloch in command of Northern Texas at Bonham. All my orders on the commissary and quartermaster's departments were signed by me as Capt. C. S. A. and duly honored.

Around Bonham I did scout service for Gen. McCulloch, and in November he sent me with a very flattering letter to report to Gen. E. Kirby Smith, at Shreveport, Louisiana, the headquarters of the Trans-Mississippi department. Capts. Jarrette and Poole were at Shreveport and Gen. Smith gave us minute orders for a campaign against the cotton thieves and speculators who infested the Mississippi river bottom. An expedition to get rid of these was planned by Gen. Smith with Capt. Poole commanding one company, myself the other, and Capt. Jarrette over us both.

Five miles from Tester's ferry on Bayou Macon we met a cotton train convoyed by 50 cavalry. We charged them on sight. The convoy got away with ten survivors, but every driver was shot, and four cotton buyers who were close behind in an ambulance were hung in a cotton gin near at hand. They had $180,000 on them, which, with the cotton and wagons, was sent back to Bastrop in charge of Lieut. Greenwood.

A more exciting experience was mine at Bayou Monticello, a stream that was deeper than it looked. Observing a cotton train on a plantation across the bayou, I called to my men to follow me and plunged in.

Seeing me floundering in the deep water, however, they went higher up to a bridge, and when I landed I found myself alone. I was hard pressed for a time, till they came up and relieved me. There were 52 soldiers killed here. Other charges near Goodrich's Landing and at Omega put an end to the cotton speculation in that locality.

The Confederate army in that section was not well armed, and our company, each man with a pair of dragoon pistols and a Sharpe's rifle, was the envy of the Southern army. Gen. Kirby Smith told me he had not seen during the war a band so well armed. Consequently when, in February, 1864, Gen. Marmaduke sent to Gen. Shelby for an officer and 40 of the best mounted and best armed men he had, it was but natural that Shelby's adjutant-general, John N. Edwards, should recommend a part of the Missouri boys, and told me to select my men and report to Gen. Shelby, who in turn ordered me to report for special service to Gen. Marmaduke at Warren, Ark.

Only twenty, and a beardless boy, Gen. Marmaduke looked me over rather dubiously, as I thought, but finally told me what he wanted—to find out whether or not it was true that Gen. Steele, at Little Rock, was preparing to move against Price at Camden, and to make the grand round of the picket posts from Warren to the Mississippi river, up the Arkansas to Pine Bluff and Little Rock, and returning by way of the western outpost at Hot Springs.

We were to intercept all messages between Price and Marmaduke, and govern our movements by their contents.

About half way between Pine Bluff and Little Rock we came

up with a train of wagons, followed by an ambulance carrying several women and accompanied by mounted Federal soldiers. The soldiers got away into Pine Bluff, but we captured the wagons and ambulance, but finding nothing of importance let them proceed.

We made a thorough examination of the interior of Little Rock, and satisfied ourselves that no movement on Price was imminent, and were on our way out before we became involved in a little shooting match with the patrol, from which no harm resulted to our side, however, except a shot in my leg.

Years afterward, in prison, I learned from Senator Cushman Kellogg Davis, of Minnesota, that he was one of the officers who galloped into Pine Bluff ahead of us that day. He was at that time on the staff of the judge advocate general, and they were on their way into Pine Bluff to hold a court-martial. The women were, as they had said, the wives of some of the officers.

Senator Davis was among the prominent Minnesotans who worked for our parole, although he did not live to see it accomplished.

16

A Clash with Apaches

In May, 1864, Col. George S. Jackson and a force of about 300, myself among the number, were sent across the staked plains into Colorado to intercept some wagon trains, and to cut the transcontinental telegraph line from Leavenworth to San Francisco. We cut the line and found the trains, but empty, and on our return were met at the Rio Grande by orders to detail a party to cross the continent on a secret mission for the Confederate states.

Two vessels of the Alabama type, built in British waters, were to be delivered at Victoria, B. C., and a secret service officer named Kennedy, who was entrusted with the papers, was given an escort of twenty men, including myself, Capt. Jarrette and other veteran scouts.

While on this expedition we had a brief tilt with Comanches, but in the country which Gen. Crook afterward fought over inch by inch, we had a real Indian fight with Apache Mojaves which lasted through two days and the night between practically without cessation.

We had a considerable advantage in weapons, but the reds were pestiferous in spite of that, and they kept us busy for fully 36 hours plugging them at every opportunity. How many Indians we killed I do not know, as we had no time or curiosity to stop and count them. They wounded some of our horses and we had to abandon one wagon, but we did not lose a man.

From El Paso we went down through Chihuahua and Sonora to Guaymas, where the party split up, Capt. Jarrette going up the mainland, while Kennedy and I, with three men, took a boat to San Francisco, disguised as Mexican miners. We were not detected, and then traveled by stage to Puget Sound, sailing for Victoria, as nearly as I have since been able to locate it, about where Seattle now is. On our arrival at Victoria, however, we found that Lee had surrendered at Appomattox and the war was at an end.

For a long time I was accused of the killing of several people at Centralia, in September, 1864, but I think my worst enemies now concede that it is impossible for me to have been there at the time.

Another spectre that rose to haunt my last days in prison, and long stood between my parole and final pardon, was the story of one John McMath, a corporal in an Indiana cavalry company, in Pleasanton's command, that I had maltreated him when he lay wounded on the battle field close by the Big Blue, near my old home in Jackson county. McMath says this occurred Oct. 23,

1863. It is true that I was in Missouri on that date, but McMath's regiment was not, nor Pleasanton's command, and the war department records at Washington show that he was injured in a fight at the Big Blue Oct. 23, 1864—a full year later—much as he says I hurt him. This was eleven months after I had left Missouri and while I was 1,500 miles away, yet this hideous charge was brought to the attention of Chief Justice Start, of Minnesota, in 1896 by a Minneapolis newspaper.

In his "Noted Guerrillas," Maj. John N. Edwards wrote:

"Lee's surrender at Appomattox found Cole Younger at Los Angeles, trying the best he could to earn a livelihood and live at peace with all the world. The character of this man to many has been a curious study, but to those who knew him well there is nothing about it of mystery or many-sidedness. An awful provocation drove him into the army. He was never a bloodthirsty or a merciless man. He was brave to recklessness, desperate to rashness, remarkable for terrible prowess in battle; but he was never known to kill a prisoner. On the contrary, there are alive today (1877) fully 200 Federal soldiers who owe their lives to Cole Younger, a man whose father had been cruelly murdered, whose mother had been hounded to her death, whose family had been made to endure the torment of a ferocious persecution, and whose kith and kin, even to remote degrees, were plundered and imprisoned. His brother James did not go into the war until 1864, and was a brave, dauntless, high-spirited boy who never killed a soldier in his life save in fair and open battle. Cole was a fair-haired, amiable, generous man, devoted in his friendships and true to his word and to comradeship. In intrepidity he was never surpassed. In battle he never had those to go where he would not follow, aye, where he would not gladly lead. On his body today there are the scars of thirty-six wounds. He was a Guerrilla and a giant among a band of Guerrillas, but he was one among five hundred who only killed in open and honorable battle. As great as had been his provocation, he never murdered; as brutal as

had been the treatment of every one near and dear to him, he refused always to take vengeance on those who were innocent of
the wrongs and who had taken no part in the deeds which drove
him, a boy, into the ranks of the Guerrillas, but he fought as a
soldier who fights for a cause, a creed, an idea, or for glory. He
was a hero and he was merciful."

17

The Edicts of Outlawry

While I was on the Pacific slope, April 8, 1865, to be exact, the
state of Missouri adopted what is known to the disgrace of its author as the Drake constitution. Confederate soldiers and sympa-
thizers were prohibited from practicing any profession, preaching the gospel, acting as deacon in a church, or doing various
other things, under penalty of a fine not less than $500 or impris-
onment in the county jail not less than six months. Section 4 of
Article 11 gave amnesty to union soldiers for their acts after Jan.
1, 1861, but held Confederates responsible for acts done either as
soldiers or citizens, and Section 12 provided for the indictment,
trial and punishment of persons accused of crime in counties
other than the one where the offense was committed.

The result of this was that Missourians were largely barred by
law from holding office and the state was overrun with "carpet-
bag" office-holders, many of whom came from Kansas, and during the war had been freebooters and bushwhackers up and
down the Kansas border.

Organizing a posse from men like themselves, sheriffs or others pretending to be sheriffs would take their mobs, rout men out
of their beds at night under service of writs, on which the only
return ever made was a pistol shot somewhere in the darkness,

THE STORY OF COLE YOUNGER

maybe in the victim's dooryard, perhaps in some lonely country road.

Visiting for a time with my uncle on the Pacific slope, I returned to Jackson county in the fall of 1865 to pick up the scattered ends of a ruined family fortune. I was 21, and no man of my age in Missouri, perhaps, had better prospects, if I had been unmolested. Mother had been driven to a refuge in a cabin on one of our farms, my brother Jim had been away during the last few months of the war fighting in the army, and had been taken prisoner in Quantrill's last fight at Wakefield's house near Smiley, Ky. He was taken to the military prison at Alton, Ill., and was released in the fall of 1865, coming home within a few days of my return.

Our faithful negro servant, "Aunt Suse," had been hung up in the barn in a vain endeavor to make her reveal the whereabouts of my mother's sons and money; my dead father's fortune had been stolen and scattered to the winds; but our farms were left, and had I been given an opportunity to till them in peace it would have saved four wasted lives.

In the summer of 1866 the governor of Kansas made a requisition on the governor of Missouri for 300 men, naming them, who had taken part in the attacks on Lawrence and other Kansas towns.

Attorneys in Independence had decided that they would defend, free of charge, for any offense except murder, any of the Jackson county boys who would give themselves up. No one did more than I to assemble the boys at Blue Springs for a meeting to consider such course.

It was while at this that I saw Jesse James for the first time in my life, so that sets at rest all the wild stories that have been told about our meeting as boys and joining Quantrill. Frank James and I had seen service together, and Frank was a good soldier, too. Jesse, however, did not enter the service until after I had gone South in the fall of 1863, and when I saw him early in the summer of 1866 he was still suffering from the shot through the lung he had received in the last battle in Johnson county in May, 1865.

The spectre of Paola now rose to haunt me. Although all the guerrillas knew who had killed young Judy, his father had secured my indictment in Kansas on the charge of murdering his son. Judy, who had returned to Missouri as the appointed sheriff of Cass county, had a posse prepared to serve a writ for me in its usual way—a night visit and then the pistol or the rope.

I consulted with old ex-Governor King at Richmond, who had two sons in the Federal army, one of whom I had captured during the war, although he did not know it at the time, and with Judge Tutt of this district.

Judge Tutt said there was no sheriff in this vicinity who would draw a jury that would give me a fair trial. If I should so make oath he, as judge, would appoint a jury commissioner who would summon a jury that would give me a fair trial, but he was confident that as soon as he did so mob law would be invoked before I could go to trial.

One man had been taken from the train and hung at Warrensburg and there had been many like offenses against former Confederate soldiers.

Judy had no legal rights in Jackson county, but in spite of that his posse started for the Younger farm one night to take me. George Belcher, a Union soldier, but not in sympathy with mob law, heard of Judy's plans, and through Sam Colwell and Zach Cooper, neighbors, I was warned in the evening of the intended raid. When they came I was well out of reach on my way to the home of my great-uncle, Thomas Fristoe, in Howard county.

Judy and his mob searched the house in vain, but they put up for a midnight supper which they compelled the faithful "Aunt Suse" to provide, and left disappointed.

Judy and his Kansas indictment were the entering wedge in a wasted life. But for him and his mob law Mr. and Mrs. Cole

Younger, for there was a dear sweetheart awaiting my return, might have been happy and prosperous residents of Jackson county from 1866 to this day.

It was while I was visiting my great-uncle in Howard county that there took place at Liberty the first of a long string of bank and train robberies, all of which were usually attributed either to the Younger brothers, or to some of their friends, and which we were unable to come out and successfully refute for two reasons, first the bringing down of a storm about the heads of those who had sheltered us; and second, giving such pursuers as Judy and his posse fresh clues to our whereabouts.

18

Not All Black

From the mass of rubbish that has been written about the guerrilla there is little surprise that the popular conception of him should be a fiendish, bloodthirsty wretch.

Yet he was, in many cases, if not in most, a man who had been born to better things, and who was made what he was by such outrages as Osceola, Palmyra, and a hundred other raids less famous, but not less infamous, that were made by Kansans into Missouri during the war.

When the war ceased those of the guerrillas who were not hung or shot, or pursued by posses till they found the hand of man turned against them at every step, settled down to become good citizens in the peaceful walks of life, and the survivors of Quantrill's band may be pardoned, in view of the black paint that has been devoted to them, in calling attention to the fact that of the members of Quantrill's command who have since been entrusted with public place not one has ever betrayed his trust.

John C. Hope was for two terms sheriff of Jackson county, Mo., in which is Kansas City, and Capt. J. M. Tucker was sheriff at Los Angeles, California. Henry Porter represented one of the Jackson county districts in the state legislature, removed to Texas, where he was made judge of the county court, and is now, I understand, a judge of probate in the state of Washington. "Pink" Gibson was for several years county judge in Johnson county; Harry Ogden served the state of Louisiana as lieutenant-governor and as one of its congressmen. Capt. J. C. Lea was for many years instructor in the military department of the University of New Mexico, and, I believe, is there yet. Jesse Hamblett was marshal at Lexington, and W. H. Gregg, who was Quantrill's first lieutenant, has been thought well enough of to be a deputy sheriff under the administration of a Republican. Jim Hendricks, deputy sheriff of Lewis and Clark county, Montana, is another, but to enumerate all the men of the old band who have held minor places would be wearisome.

19

A Duel and an Auction

I left Missouri soon after Judy's raid for Louisiana, spending three months with Capt. J. C. Lea on what was known as the Widow Amos' farm on Fortune fork, Tensas parish. We then rented the Bass farm on Lake Providence, in Carroll parish, where I stayed until 1867, when chills and fever drove me north to Missouri. When the bank at Russellville, Ky., was robbed, which has been laid to us, I was with my uncle, Jeff Younger, in St. Clair county, and Jim and Bob were at home here in Lee's Summit.

At the time of the Richmond and Savannah, Mo., bank robberies, in which, according to newspapers and sensationalists, I was largely concerned, I was living on the Bass plantation, three miles below Lake Providence, in Louisiana. Capt. J. C. and Frank Lea, of Roswell, N. M., and Tom Lea, of Independence, Mo., were living in the same house with me, any one of whom will vouch for the truth of my statement that I was not anywhere near either of these towns at the time of the robberies in question, but was with them at the plantation referred to above. Furthermore, right here I want to state, and I will take my oath solemnly that what I say is the truth, and *nothing but the truth, notwithstanding all the accusations that have been made against me, I never, in all my life, had anything whatever to do with robbing any bank in the state of Missouri.* I could prove that I was not in the towns where banks were robbed in Missouri, at the time that the raids took place, and in many instances that I was thousands of miles away.

In the fall of 1868 Jim and Bob went with me to Texas. Mother's health had failed perceptibly, the result in a large measure of her exposure at the time the militia forced her to burn her house, and we sought to make her a home in a milder climate in the southwest. The next two or three years we spent there gathering and driving cattle, my sister joining us and keeping house for us at Syene, Dallas county, where we made our headquarters.

I was at Austin, Texas, when the Gallatin, Mo., bank was robbed; another crime of which we have been accused by the romancers, though never, so far as I know, by the authorities.

In 1870 and 1871 Jim was deputy sheriff of Dallas county.

Jim and Bob sang in the church choir there until 1872, when Bob, who was only seventeen, and in love with one of the local belles, felt keenly the obloquy attaching to the accusation that his brother Cole had robbed the Kansas City fair, and left Dallas.

One of the lies that had been published broadcast concerning me is that I killed five men and shot five others in a row over a "jobbed" horse race in Louisiana. There is this much truth about it—there was a jobbed race, and after it I fought a duel, but not over the race.

In the crowd that was present at the race was one Capt. Jim White, to whom I had sent word during the war that when I met him again he would have to apologize or fight because of circulating some scandal about a young woman friend of mine.

White introduced himself to me after this race, where a friend of mine had been swindled out of considerable money, and we went over to a neighboring plantation to shoot it out. At the first fire his right arm was shattered at the shoulder. He thought he was fatally hurt, and so did I at first, and he called me over and said:

"Captain Younger, whether I die or not, I want to shake hands with you as a friend. I have had some differences of this sort with others and came out all right; people have sneered at my success and said, 'Wait till Cap'n Younger gets at you. He'll fix you!' So I finally made up my mind to fight you, right or wrong."

I told my friend who owned the plantation to take care of White, and I went to Texas to make in the cattle business some of the money I had lost trying to raise cotton. The next year I was over in Mississippi at a dance, and a young lady asked to be introduced to me.

Her name was White, and we had not talked long before she said:

"Mother says you've made a man of father."

Captain White had crossed the river, quit his drinking associates, but I have never seen him since the day we shot it out.

This duel gave Cole Younger a reputation in that section which was of value to a poor preacher's widow near Bayou Macon some time later.

There was to be a sale of the property and effects of the Widow Hurley. I attended the sale, hitched my horse in the barn lot and was walking across the garden at the back of the house toward an open space, where the crowd was gathered waiting for the auctioneer to open the sale. As I walked I came upon Mrs. Hurley, crying. "Good morning, Mrs. Hurley," I said, "I am sorry to see you in tears; what is the trouble?"

She explained that her husband had mortgaged the property and stock before his death and she had not been able to lift it, and they were about to be taken away from her. I asked her what the amount of the indebtedness was, and she told me $80. I took the money out of my pocket and gave it to her, and told her to bid it in when the time came, and I gave her the signal.

Asbury Humphreys, who was the auctioneer, knew me from the story of the duel, and before he began I told him he would have to put the property all up at once.

Some of the fellows from over on the river wanted the cows and hogs put up separately, so they could pick out what they wanted, and Asbury declared he was afraid to change the plan for the sale. They would not let him live there if he did.

"Well, Asbury," I said, "I'm going to be down beside the wagon where I can see you and you can see me, and when I give you the sign you knock the property down or I'll have use for this pistol."

I had not had time to coach Mrs. Hurley, so she made it somewhat embarrassing for Asbury. There was kicking enough when he announced that he had decided to put all the goods up in a lump, but he looked down where I was learning against the wheel of his wagon and stood pat.

When he called for bids Mrs. Hurley bid her whole $80. I had not taken the precaution to tell her to start it lower, and there were now only two ways out of it, either to give her more money or have it knocked down to her right there.

I decided that the shortest way out of it was to have Asbury knock it down to her then and there, so I gave him the sign.

I had to protect Asbury from the crowd for a few minutes, but there was no harm done to any one. Mrs. Hurley had her goods, and the creditor had his money, and I was out $80, while Asbury's reliability as an auctioneer was called into some question until his position in the matter was fully understood.

20

Laurels Unsought

Although every book purporting to narrate the lives of the Younger brothers has told of the Liberty robbery, and implied that we had a part in it, the Youngers were not suspected at that time, nor for a long time afterward. It was claimed by people of Liberty that they positively recognized among the robbers Oll Shepherd, "Red" Monkers and "Bud" Pence, who had seen service with Quantrill. Jim White and J. F. Edmunson were arrested in St. Joseph, but were promptly released, their preliminary examination failing to connect them with the raid in any way.

In October of that year a bank at Lexington, Mo., was robbed of $2,000, but so far as I know it was never connected with the Younger brothers in any way until 1880, when J. W. Buel published his "Border Bandits."

March 2, 1867, the bank at Savannah, Mo., was raided, but the five who did this were identified, and there were no Younger boys in the party. This raid was accompanied by bloodshed, Judge McLain, the banker, being shot, though not fatally.

May 23 of that year the bank at Richmond, Mo., was raided, Mayor Shaw was killed, and the robbers raided the jail, where were confined a number of prisoners whose arrest, it was claimed, was due to their sympathy with secession. Jailer Griffin and his 15-year-old son were killed there. Warrants were issued for a number of the old guerrillas, including Allen Parmer, afterward the husband of Susie James, although he was working in Kansas City at the time, and proved an absolute alibi. No warrant was issued for the Youngers, but subsequent historians (?) have, inferentially at least, accused us of taking part, but as I said before, there is no truth in the accusation.

The bank at Russellville, Ky., was raided March 20, 1868, and among the raiders was a man who gave his name as Colburn, who the detectives have endeavored to make it appear was Cole Younger. Having served in Kentucky with Quantrill, Jim Younger and Frank James were well known through that state, and it being known that the previous bank robberies in Missouri were charged to ex-guerrillas, similar conclusions were at once drawn by the Louisville sleuths who were put on the case. Jim and John were at home at Lee's Summit.

June 3, 1871, Obocock Bros.' bank at Corydon, Iowa, was robbed of $40,000 by seven men in broad daylight. The romancers have connected Jim and me with that, when as a matter of fact I was in Louisiana, Jim and Bob were at Dallas, and John was in California.

April 29, 1872, the day that the bank at Columbia, Ky., was raided and the cashier, R. A. C. Martin, killed I was at Neosho Falls, Kansas, with a drove of cattle.

September 26 of the same year the cash-box of the Kansas City fair was stolen. A full statement as to my whereabouts during the day is given in a letter appended hereto, which also shows that it would have been impossible for me to be present at the wrecking of the Rock Island train in Adair county, Iowa, July 21, 1873; the hold-up of the Malvern stage near the Gaines place Jan. 15, 1874; the Ste. Genevieve bank robbery May 27, 1873, or the Iron Mountain train robbery at Gad's Hill, Mo., Jan. 31, 1874. It was charged that Arthur McCoy or A. C. McCoy and myself had been participants in the Gad's Hill affair and the two stage robberies.

Nov. 15, 1874, I wrote a letter to my brother-in-law, Lycargus

A. Jones, which was published in part in the Pleasant Hill Review Nov. 26, the editor having in the meantime inquired into the statements of facts and satisfied himself of their truth. The parts of this letter now relevant are as follows:

Cass County, Nov. 15, 1874.

Dear Curg: You may use this letter in your own way. I will give you this outline and sketch of my whereabouts and actions at the time of certain robberies with which I am charged. At the time of the Gallatin bank robbery I was gathering cattle in Ellis county, Texas; cattle that I bought from Pleas Taylor and Rector. This can be proved by both of them; also by Sheriff Barkley and fifty other respectable men of that county. I brought the cattle to Kansas that fall and remained in St. Clair county until February. I then went to Arkansas and returned to St. Clair county about the first of May. I went to Kansas, where our cattle were, in Woodson county, at Col. Ridge's. During the summer I was either in St. Clair, Jackson or Kansas, but as there was no robbery committed that summer it makes no difference where I was.

The gate at the fair grounds was robbed that fall. I was in Jackson county at the time. I left R. P. Rose's that morning, went down the Independence road, stopped at Dr. Noland's, and got some pills. Brother John was with me. I went through Independence and from there to Ace Webb's. There I took dinner and then went to Dr. L. W. Twyman's. Stayed there until after supper, then went to Silas Hudspeth's and stayed all night. This was the day the gate was robbed at Kansas City. Next day John and I went to Kansas City. We crossed the river at Blue Mills and went up on the other side. Our business there was to see E. P. West. He was not at home, but the family will remember that we were there. We crossed on the bridge, stayed in the city all night and the next morning we rode up through the city. I met several of my friends. Among them was Bob Hudspeth. We then returned to the Six-Mile country by the way of Independence. At Big Blue we met Jas. Chiles and had a long talk with him. I saw several friends that were standing at or near the gate, and they all said that they didn't know any of the party that did the robbing. Neither John nor myself was accused of the crime until several days after. My name would never have been used in connection with the affair had not Jesse W. James, for some cause best known to himself, published in the Kansas City Times a letter stating that John, he and myself were accused of the robbery. Where he got his authority I don't know, but one thing I do know, he had none from me. We were not on good terms at the time, nor have we been for several years. From that time on mine and John's names have been connected with the James brothers. John hadn't seen either of them for eighteen months before his death. And as for A. C. McCoy, John never saw him in his life. I knew A. C. McCoy during the war, but have never seen him since, notwithstanding the Appleton City paper says he has been with us in that county for two years. Now if any respectable man in that county will say he ever saw A. C. McCoy with me or John I will say no more; or if any reliable man will say that he ever saw any one with us who suited the description of A. C. McCoy then I will be silent and never more plead innocence.

Poor John, he has been hunted down and shot like a wild beast, and never was a boy more innocent. But there is a day coming when the secrets of all hearts will be laid open before that All-seeing Eye, and every act of our lives will be scrutinized; then will his skirts be white as the driven snow, while those of his accusers will be doubly dark.

I will come now to the Ste. Genevieve robbery. At that time I was in St. Clair county, Mo. I do not remember the date, but Mr. Murphy, one of our neighbors, was sick about that time, and I sat up with him regularly, where I met with some of his neighbors every day. Dr. L. Lewis was his physician.

As to the Iowa train robbery, I have forgotten the day, I was also in St. Clair county, Mo., at that time, and had the pleasure of attending preaching the evening previous to the robbery at Monegaw Springs. There were fifty or a hundred persons there who will testify in any court that John and I were there. I will give you the names of some of them: Simeon C. Bruce, John S. Wilson, James Van Allen, Rev. Mr. Smith and lady. Helvin Fickle and wife of Greenton Valley were attending the springs at that time, and either of them will testify to the above, for John and I sat in front of Mr. Smith while he was preaching and was in his company for a few moments, together with his wife and Mr. and Mrs. Fickle, after service. They live at Greenton Valley, Lafayette county, Mo., and their evidence would be taken in the court of heaven. As there was no other robbery committed until January, I will come to that time. About the last of December, 1873, I arrived in Carroll parish, Louisiana. I stayed there until the 8th of February, 1874. Brother and I stayed at Wm. Dickerson's, near Floyd. During the time the Shreveport stage and the Hot Springs stage were robbed; also the Gad's Hill robbery.

THOMAS COLEMAN YOUNGER

On reading since my release the pretended history of my life I find that I was wrong in stating that there was no robbery during the summer of 1872, the bank at Columbia, Ky., having been raided April 29 of that year. I had not heard of that when I wrote the letter of 1874, and to correct any misapprehension that might be created by omitting it I will say that at that time I was at Neosho, Kansas, with a drove of cattle, which I sold to Maj. Ray.

It was immediately following the Rock Island robbery at Adair, Iowa, that there first appeared a deliberate enlistment of some local papers in Missouri to connect us with this robbery. New York and Chicago as well as St. Paul and Minneapolis papers did not connect the Youngers with the crime, and three days after the robbery these papers had it that the robbers had been followed into Nodaway county, Missouri, while we were at

Monegaw Springs all that time. Besides those mentioned in my 1874 letter, Marshall P. Wright's affidavit that he showed Jim and me at Monegaw Springs the morning paper containing the account of the robbery the next morning after it took place, was presented to Gov. Clough of Minnesota in 1898.

It is 250 miles or more and no cross lines of railroad existed to facilitate our passage, so it would be impossible for any one to have made the trip. The shortest rail lines are roundabout, via St. Joseph and Kansas City, so it will be apparent that I could not have been at the Rock Island wreck.

21

The Truth about John Younger

John, my brother, was fourteen when the war closed and Bob under twelve. One day in January, 1866, John, Bob and my mother drove into Independence to mill, and to do other errands in town, one of which was to get one of my pistols fixed.

A young fellow named Gillcreas, who had served in the militia and was several years John's senior, hit the boy with a piece of mackerel, and warm words ensued.

"Why don't you shoot him?" shouted Bob from the wagon.

John told the fellow if Cole were there he would not dare do that, and Gillcreas said Cole should be in prison, and all Quantrill's men with him. Gillcreas went away, but returned to the attack, this time armed with a heavy slungshot. In the meantime John had gotten the pistol which had been in the wagon. Gillcreas came up to resume the fight and John shot him dead. The slungshot was found with the thong twined about Gillcreas' wrist.

The coroner's jury acquitted John, and there were many people in Independence who felt that he had done just right.

When I went to Louisiana in 1868 John went with me, afterward accompanying me to Texas. Clerking in a store in Dallas, he became associated with some young fellows of reckless habits and drank somewhat.

One day, while they were all in a gay mood, John shot the pipe out of the mouth of a fellow named Russell. Russell jumped up and ran out of the room.

"Don't kill him," shouted the crowd in ridicule, and John fired several random shots to keep up the scare.

Russell swore out a warrant for John's arrest, and next morning, Jan. 17, 1871, Capt. S. W. Nichols, the sheriff, and John McMahon came up to the house to arrest him. John made no resistance and invited the officers to breakfast, but they declined and went back down town. Thompson McDaniels called John's attention to the fact that a guard had been stationed over his horses, and they walked down town together. Tom and John drank some whisky, and while they were waiting Nichols and his party had taken on some too.

"What did you put a guard over my horses for?" asked John, when he entered the room where Nichols was.

"I did not put any guard over your horses," replied Nichols.

"You're a —— liar," continued John, "I saw them there myself."

At this another Russell, a brother of the one whose pipe had been shot out of his mouth, opened fire on John and wounded him in the arm. Thomp. McDaniels shot Capt. Nichols, and in the melee McMahon was shot, as far as I have ever been able to learn, by my brother.

John and McDaniels went out, took the officers' horses and rode to Missouri.

It developed after the shooting that the same Russell who had opened fire on John had placed the guard over the horses, and that Capt. Nichols had not known of it.

I was away in Louisiana at the time, but on my return several

attorneys offered to defend John if he would return for trial, but
after a visit at the home of our uncle in California he returned to
Missouri in the winter of 1873 and 1874, just in time to be suspected of the train robbery at Gad's Hill, on the Iron Mountain
road.

John and Jim were visiting at the home of our friend,
Theodoric Snuffer, at Monegaw Springs, St. Clair county.

Man-hunters had sought us there on a previous occasion
when we were all four there. We had come upon the party of 15
suddenly, and I covered them with a shot-gun, demanded their
surrender, and explaining that we had not robbed anybody, and
wanted to be treated as decent citizens, approached by officers
of the law in the regular manner if we were accused, restored
their arms to them, and they went back to Osceola.

March 11, 1874, J. W. Whicher, a Pinkerton detective from
Chicago, who had been sent out to arrest Frank and Jesse James
at Kearney, was found dead in the road near Independence, and
W. J. Allen, otherwise known as Capt. Lull, a St. Louis plain-
clothes cop who passed by the name of Wright, and an Osceola
boy named Ed. Daniels, who was a deputy sheriff with an ambi-
tion to shine as a sleuth, rode out to find Jim and Bob at the
Springs.

The boys, advised of their coming by a negro servant, sought
to convince them, as we had the earlier posse, that they could
not have had anything to do with the affair at Gad's Hill. But
Allen, remembering the recent fate of Whicher, drew his pistol
and shot John in the neck. John returned the fire and killed
Daniels and took after Allen. Side by side the horses galloped,
John firing at the detective till he fell from the saddle mortally
wounded. John turned to ride back to where Jim was, when he
toppled from his saddle and was dead in a few minutes.

The St. Louis detective had fled at the first fire, and lived to
tell graphic stories of how it all happened, although he was really
too busy getting out to know anything about it.

22

Amnesty Bill Fails

The killing of Lull, Daniels and Whicher within a single week was undoubtedly exasperating to the head of the Pinkerton agency, and had he not been personally embittered thereby he probably would not have avenged it so terribly.

In the next January, 1875, a posse of Pinkerton men and others, guided by Daniel H. Asker, a neighbor of the James boys, proceeded to their home near Kearney and threw a bomb into the house where the family was seated. An eight-year-old half-brother of Frank and Jesse was killed, their mother, Mrs. Samuels, had one arm torn off, and other members of the family were more or less injured. But Frank and Jesse were not taken.

There had been a feeling among many people in the state even before that these detectives were unjustly pursuing some of the Confederate soldiers, and I have been told since that Gov. Silas Woodson was on the eve of interfering with Pinkerton's men when news came that two of them had been killed in an encounter with John and Jim Younger.

At any rate the death of the innocent little Samuels boy made still more pronounced this feeling against the operations of the detectives, and in favor of the members of the Confederate army who had been outlawed by Fremont, Halleck, Ewing and the Drake constitution, ungenerously, to say the least.

This feeling found definite expression shortly after the raid on the Samuels home in the introduction of a bill in the Missouri legislature offering amnesty to the Younger and James brothers by name, and others who had been outlawed with them by proclamation, from all their acts during the war, and promising them a fair trial on any charge against them arising after the war.

The bill was introduced in the house by the late General Jeff Jones, of Callaway county, where my brothers and myself had many friends, and was, in the main, as follows:

"Whereas, by the 4th section of the 11th article of the Constitution of Missouri, all persons in the military service of the United States or who acted under the authority thereof in this state, are relieved from all civil liability and all criminal punishment for all acts done by them since the 1st day of January, A.D. 1861; and,

"Whereas, By the 12th section of the said 11th article of said constitution provision is made by which, under certain circumstances, may be seized, transported to, indicted, tried and punished in distant counties, any confederate under ban of despotic displeasure, thereby contravening the Constitution of the United States and every principle of enlightened humanity; and,

"Whereas, Such discrimination evinces a want of manly generosity and statesmanship on the part of the party imposing, and of courage and manhood on the part of the party submitting tamely thereto; and,

"Whereas, Under the outlawry pronounced against Jesse W. James, Frank James, Coleman Younger, James Younger and others, who gallantly periled their lives and their all in defense of their principles, they are of necessity made desperate, driven as they are from the fields of honest industry, from their friends, their families, their homes and their country, they can know no law but the law of self-preservation, nor can have no respect for and feel no allegiance to a government which forces them to the very acts it professes to deprecate, and then offers a bounty for their apprehension, and arms foreign mercenaries with power to capture and kill them; and,

"Whereas, Believing these men too brave to be mean, too generous to be revengeful, and too gallant and honorable to betray a friend or break a promise; and believing further that most, if not all of the offenses with which they are charged have been committed by others, and perhaps by those pretending to hunt them, or by their confederates; that their names are and have been used to divert suspicion from and thereby relieve the actual perpetrators; that the return of these men to their homes and friends would have the effect of greatly lessening crime in our state by turning public attention to the real criminals, and that common justice, sound policy and true statesmanship alike demand that amnesty should be extended to all alike of both parties for all acts done or charged to have been done during the war; therefore, be it

"*Resolved by the House of Representatives, the Senate concurring therein*, That the Governor of the state be, and he is hereby requested to issue his proclamation notifying the said Jesse W. James, Frank James, Coleman Younger, and James Younger and others, that full and complete amnesty and pardon will be granted them for all acts charged or committed by them during the late civil war, and inviting them peacefully to return to their respective homes in this state and there quietly to remain, submitting themselves to such proceedings as may be instituted against them by the courts for all offenses charged to have been committed since said war, promising and guaranteeing to each of them full protection and a fair trial therein, and that full protection shall be given them from the time of their entrance into the state and his notice thereof under said proclamation and invitation."

It was approved by Attorney-General Hockaday, favorably reported by a majority of the committee on criminal jurisprudence, but while it was pending Farmer Askew, who had piloted the detectives in their raid on the Samuels residence, was called to his door at night and shot and killed by unknown parties.

The bill was beaten, Democrats and Confederate soldiers voting against it.

For myself, the only charge against me was the unwarranted one of the killing of young Judy during the war, but the failure of the bill left us still under the ban of outlawry.

23

Belle Starr

One of the richest mines for the romancers who have pretended to write the story of my life was the fertile imagination of Belle Starr, who is now dead, peace to her ashes.

These fairy tales have told how the "Cherokee maiden fell in love with the dashing captain." As a matter of fact, Belle Starr was not a Cherokee. Her father was John Shirley, who during the war had a hotel at Carthage, Mo. In the spring of 1864, while I was in Texas, I visited her father, who had a farm near Syene, in Dallas county. Belle Shirley was then 14, and there were two or three brothers smaller.

The next time I saw Belle Shirley was in 1868, in Bates county, Mo. She was then the wife of Jim Reed, who had been in my company during the war, and she was at the home of his mother. This was about three months before the birth of her eldest child, Pearl Reed, afterward known as Pearl Starr, after Belle's second husband.

In 1871, while I was herding cattle in Texas, Jim Reed and his wife, with their two children, came back to her people. Reed had run afoul of the Federal authorities for passing counterfeit money at Los Angeles and had skipped between two days. Belle told her people she was tired roaming the country over and wanted to settle down at Syene. Mrs. Shirley wanted to give them part of the farm, and knowing my influence with the father, asked me to intercede in behalf of the young folks. I did, and he set them up on the farm, and I cut out a lot of the calves from one of my two herds and left with them.

That day Belle Reed told me her troubles, and that night "Aunt Suse," our family servant, warned me.

"Belle's sure in love with you, Cap'n Cole," she explained. "You better be careful."

With that hint I thereafter evaded the wife of my former comrade in arms.

Reed was killed a few years later after the robbery of the stage near San Antonio, and Belle married again, this time Tom Starr or Sam Starr.

Later she came to Missouri and traveled under the name of Younger, boasted of an intimate acquaintance with me, served time in state prison, and at this time declared that she was my wife, and that the girl Pearl was our child.

At this time I had no knowledge of any one named Belle Starr, and I was at a loss as to her identity until the late Lillian Lewis, the actress, who was related to some very good friends of our family, inquired about her on one of her tours through the southwest. Visiting me in prison, she told me that Belle Starr was the daughter of John Shirley, and then for the first time had I any clue as to her identity.

Her story was a fabrication, inspired undoubtedly by the notoriety it would give her through the Cherokee nation, where the name of Younger was widely known, whether fortunately or unfortunately.

24

"Captain Dykes"

The winter that the amnesty bill was before the Missouri legislature I spent in Florida, with the exception of a short trip to Cuba. I was the greater part of the time at Lake City. I sent Bob to school at William and Mary college, but the same proud spirit that caused him to leave Dallas in 1872 impelled him to leave college when his fellow students began to connect his uncommon name with that of the notorious Missouri outlaw, Cole Younger. He rejoined me in Florida. I was "Mr. Dykes," a sojourner from the north, and while I carried a pair of pistols in my belt to guard against the appearance of any of Judy's ilk, the people of Lake City never knew it until one day when the village was threatened with a race riot.

A lot of the blacks there had been members of a negro regiment and all had arms. My barber was of a different school of darkies, and the Lake City blacks determined to run him out of town. He told me of the plan, and I did not take much stock in it until one morning when I was being shaved I heard the plotters, over a bottle of whisky in an adjoining room, declaring what they were going to do. Soon after I left the shop I heard a pistol shot, and turning around to see what was the matter, I saw my barber running toward me, while the other darkies were scattering to their homes for their guns. I walked up the street a little distance with the barber, when some one called to me, and I saw that the lieutenant of this old company had us covered by his gun. I ran up to him and planting my pistol between his eyes, commanded him to drop the gun, which the barber got in a jiffy. The pistol

shot in the shop had alarmed the merchants, each of whom kept
a gun in his store, and thereafter as the blacks came to the rally-
ing place in the public square with their guns we disarmed them
quicker than it takes to tell it, and they were locked up to cool off.

After that I was dubbed "Capt." Dykes, by unanimous consent, and had to be more careful than before lest the military title should attract to me the attention of some curious investiga-
tor who would have overlooked entirely "Mr. Dykes."

The disguised outlaw became during the remainder of his
residence a leading and respected citizen. When the election was
held it was "Capt. Dykes" who was called upon to preserve order
at the polls, he, of course, having no interest as between the ri-
val candidates, and with pistols in easy reach he maintained per-
fect order during one of the most exciting elections Lake City
had ever had.

25

Eluding the Police

Bob and I had a close call with the St. Louis police in the fall of
that year. The bank at Huntington, West Virginia, was robbed the
first of September that year, and in the chase of the robbers
Thompson McDaniels, who had fought with us in the war, was
shot and fatally hurt. In his delirium he called for "Bud," and
many, among whom was Detective Bly of Louisville, thought that
he meant me, I having been known familiarly throughout the
war as "Bud" Younger. This fact has made careless writers connect Brother Bob with some of my exploits, and in his case it
served to throw suspicion on me when in fact it was probably
"Bud" or Bill McDaniels, Thompson's brother, about whom he
was raving. Bill was killed shortly before, escaping from arrest for
complicity in the Muncie train robbery.

Shortly after this Huntington affair Bob and I were coming north from Florida. We had ridden as far as Nashville, and sold our horses there, carrying the saddle pockets with us. Shortly before we reached St. Louis we met the morning papers, full of the Huntington robbery, and the statement that the robbers were headed for Missouri. Knowing that we would be watched for in St. Louis, I told Bob we would have to go through anyway. There were some farmers' families on the train from White county, Tennessee, who were moving to the big bend of the Arkansas river, the men and goods having gone on ahead by freight. We determined to get in with these people and bluff it through. As they always do at St. Louis when on the lookout, a lot of detectives boarded the train at East St. Louis and came through, but I was busy showing one of the small boys the river, and Bob had a little girl who was equally interested in the strange city before her. Gathering up a lot of the baggage of the women folks, we went through the union depot. Chief of Detectives McDonough was standing by the gate and I saw him as I passed within a few feet of him, but he made no sign. We took the women down town to the office where they got their rebates on their tickets, and then we took them back to the depot and left them, very grateful for our considerate attention, although, perhaps, we were under as deep obligations to them as they were to us, if they had known all the facts.

But I was determined to take no further chances, and told Bob to get in a hack that stood outside, and if we were stopped I would get on top and drive.

As we told the driver to go to a certain hotel we allayed the suspicion of a policeman who stood near and he made no effort to molest us. When we got around a corner and out of sight we paid the hackman and skipped out to Union, where we spent the night, and came up to Little Blue, on the Missouri Pacific, the next day.

26

Ben Butler's Money

There was no change in the situation in Missouri so far as the Younger brothers were concerned. Every daylight robbery in any part of the country, from the Alleghenies to the Rockies, was laid at our doors; we could not go out without a pair of pistols to protect ourselves from the attack of we knew not whom; and finally, after one of the young ruffians who had helped in the robbery of the Missouri Pacific express car at Otterville "confessed" that we were with the robbers we decided to make one haul, and with our share of the proceeds start life anew in Cuba, South America, or Australia.

Gen. Benjamin F. Butler, whom we preferred to call "Silver Spoons" Butler from his New Orleans experiences during the war, had a lot of money invested, we were told, in the First National bank at Northfield, Minnesota, as also had J. T. Ames, Butler's son-in-law, who had been the "carpet-bag" governor of Mississippi after the war.*

Butler's treatment of the Southerners during the war was not such as to commend him to our regard, and we felt little compunction, under the circumstances, about raiding him or his.

---

* John T. Ames was a director of the First National Bank and the brother of Adelbert Ames, who had married Benjamin Butler's daughter, Blanche, in 1870. In March, 1876, Adelbert resigned as governor of Mississippi. In September, he witnessed the bank raid while in Northfield to visit relatives and deal with matters connected with the Ames family milling business. Jesse Ames and Sons owned one-fifth of the stock in the bank.

Accordingly, about the middle of August we made up a party to visit Northfield, going north by rail. There were Jim, Bob and myself, Clell Miller, who had been accused of the Gad's Hill, Muncie, Corydon, Hot Springs and perhaps other bank and train robberies, but who had not been convicted of any of them; Bill Chadwell, a young fellow from Illinois, and three men whose names on the expedition were Pitts, Woods and Howard.

We spent a week in Minneapolis, seeing the sights, playing poker and looking around for information, after which we spent a similar period in St. Paul.

I was accounted a fairly good poker player in those days, and had won about $3,000 the winter I was in Florida, while Chadwell was one of the best that ever played the game.

We both played our last game of poker in St. Paul that week, for he was soon to die at Northfield, and in the quarter of a century that has passed since such a change has come over me that I not only have no desire to play cards, but it disgusts me even to see boys gamble with dice for cigars.

This last game was at a gambling house on East Third street, between Jackson and Robert streets, about half a block from the Merchants' hotel, where we were stopping. Guy Salisbury, who has since become a minister, was the proprietor of the gambling house, and Charles Hickson was the bartender. It was upstairs over a restaurant run by Archie McLeod, who is still in St. Paul.

Chadwell and I were nearly $300 ahead of the game when Bob came along and insisted on sitting in, and we left the table. I never would play in a game where Bob was.

Early in the last week in August we started on the preliminary work for the Northfield expedition.

27

Horace Greeley Perry

When we split up in St. Paul Howard, Woods, Jim and Clell Miller were to go to Red Wing to get their horses, while Chadwell, Pitts, Bob and myself were to go to St. Peter or Mankato, but Bob and Chadwell missed the train and they had me in a stew to know what had happened to them. We watched the papers, but could find nothing about any arrest, and Pitts and I bought our horses at St. Peter. I was known as King, and some of the fellows called me Congressman King, insisting that I bore some resemblance to Congressman William S. King of Minneapolis. I bought two horses, one from a man named Hodge and the other from a man named French, and while we were breaking them there at St. Peter I made the acquaintance of a little girl who was afterward one of the most earnest workers for our parole.

A little tot then, she said she could ride a horse, too, and reaching down I lifted her up before me, and we rode up and down. I asked her name and she said it was "Horace Greeley Perry," and I replied:

"No wonder you're such a little tot, with such a great name."

"I won't always be little," she replied. "I'm going to be a great big girl, and be a newspaper man like my pa."

"Will you still be my sweetheart then, and be my friend?" I asked her, and she declared she would, a promise I was to remind her of years later under circumstances of which I did not dream then.

Many years afterward with a party of visitors to the prison came a girl, perhaps sixteen, who registered in full "Horace Greeley Perry."

I knew there could not be two women with such a name in the world, and I reminded her of her promise, a promise which she did not remember, although she had been told how she had made friends with the bold bad man who afterwards robbed the bank at Northfield.

Very soon afterward, at the age of eighteen, I believe, she became, as she had dreamed in childhood, a "newspaper man," editing the St. Peter Journal, and to the hour of my pardon she was one of the most indefatigable workers for us.

A few years ago failing health compelled her removal from Minnesota to Idaho, and Minnesota lost one of the brightest newspaper writers and one of the best and truest women and staunchest friends that a man ever knew. Jim and I had a host of earnest advocates during the latter years of our imprisonment, but none exceeded in devotion the young woman who, as a little tot, had ridden, unknowingly, with the bandit who was so soon to be exiled for life from all his kin and friends.

28

The Northfield Raid

While Pitts and I were waiting for Bob and Chadwell we scouted about, going to Madelia and as far as the eastern part of Cottonwood county, to familiarize ourselves with the country. Finally, a few days later, the boys joined us, having bought their horses at Mankato.

We then divided into two parties and started for Northfield by somewhat different routes. Monday night, Sept. 4, our party were at Le Sueur Center, and court being in session, we had to sleep on the floor. The hotel was full of lawyers, and they, with the judge and other court attendants, had a high old time that night.

Tuesday night we were at Cordova, a little village in Le Sueur county, and Wednesday night in Millersburg, eleven miles west of Northfield. Bob and his party were then at Cannon City, to the south of Northfield. We reunited Thursday morning, Sept. 7, a little outside Northfield, west of the Cannon river.

We took a trip into town that forenoon, and I looked over the bank. We had dinner at various places and then returned to the camp. While we were planning the raid it was intended that I should be one of the party to go into the bank. I urged on the boys that whatever happened we should not shoot any one.

"What if they begin shooting at us?" some one suggested.

"Well," said Bob, "if Cap is so particular about the shooting, suppose we let him stay outside and take his chances."

So at the last minute our plans were changed, and when we started for town Bob, Pitts and Howard went in front, the plan being for them to await us in the square and enter the bank when the second detachment came up with them. Miller and I went second to stand guard at the bank, while the rest of the party were to wait at the bridge for the signal—a pistol shot— in the event they were needed. There were no saddle horses in evidence, and we calculated that we would have a considerable advantage. Wrecking the telegraph office as we left, we would get a good start, and by night would be safe beyond Shieldsville, and the next day could ride south across the Iowa line and be in comparative safety.

But between the time we broke camp and the time they reached the bridge the three who went ahead drank a quart of whisky, and there was the initial blunder at Northfield. I never knew Bob to drink before, and I did not know he was drinking that day till after it was all over.

When Miller and I crossed the bridge the three were on some dry goods boxes at the corner near the bank, and as soon as they saw us went right into the bank, instead of waiting for us to get there.

When we came up I told Miller to shut the bank door, which they had left open in their hurry. I dismounted in the street, pretending to tighten my saddle girth. J. S. Allen, whose hardware store was near, tried to go into the bank, but Miller ordered him away, and he ran around the corner, shouting:

"Get your guns, boys; they're robbing the bank."

Dr. H. M. Wheeler, who had been standing on the east side of Division street, near the Dampier house, shouted "Robbery! Robbery!" and I called to him to get inside, at the same time firing a pistol shot in the air as a signal to the three boys at the bridge that we had been discovered. Almost at this instant I heard a pistol shot in the bank. Chadwell, Woods and Jim rode up and joined us, shouting to people in the street to get inside, and firing their pistols to emphasize their commands. I do not believe they killed any one, however. I have always believed that the man Nicholas Gustavson, who was shot in the street, and who, it was said, did not go inside because he did not understand English, was hit by a glancing shot from Manning's or Wheeler's rifle. If any of our party shot him it must have been Woods.

A man named Elias Stacy, armed with a shot-gun, fired at Miller just as he was mounting his horse, filling Clell's face full of bird shot. Manning took a shot at Pitts' horse, killing it, which crippled us badly. Meantime the street was getting uncomfortably hot. Every time I saw any one with a bead on me I would drop off my horse and try to drive the shooter inside, but I could not see in every direction. I called to the boys in the bank to come out, for I could not imagine what was keeping them so long. With his second shot Manning wounded me in the thigh, and with his third he shot Chadwell through the heart. Bill fell from the saddle dead. Dr. Wheeler, who had gone upstairs in the hotel, shot Miller, and he lay dying in the street.

At last the boys who had been in the bank came out. Bob ran down the street toward Manning, who hurried into Lee & Hitchcock's store, hoping in that way to get a shot at Bob from behind.

Bob, however, did not see Wheeler, who was upstairs in the hotel behind him, and Wheeler's third shot shattered Bob's right elbow as he stood beneath the stairs. Changing his pistol to his left hand, Bob ran out and mounted Miller's mare. Howard and Pitts had at last come out of the bank. Miller was lying in the street, but we thought him still alive. I told Pitts to put him up with me, and I would pack him out, but when we lifted him I saw he was dead, and I told Pitts to lay him down again. Pitts' horse had been killed, and I told him I would hold the crowd back while he got out on foot. I stayed there pointing my pistol at any one who showed his head until Pitts had gone perhaps 30 or 40 yards, and then, putting spurs to my horse, I galloped to where he was and took him up behind me.

"What kept you so long?" I asked Pitts.

Then he told me they had been drinking and had made a botch of it inside the bank. Instead of carrying out the plan originally formed, seizing the cashier at his window and getting to the safe without interruption, they leaped right over the counter and scared Heywood at the very start. As to the rest of the affair inside the bank I take the account of a Northfield narrator:

"With a flourish of his revolver one of the robbers pointed to Joseph L. Heywood, head bookkeeper, who was acting as cashier in the absence of that official, and asked:

"'Are you the cashier?'

"'No,' replied Heywood, and the same question was put to A. E. Bunker, teller, and Frank J. Wilcox, assistant bookkeeper, each of whom made the same reply.

"'You are the cashier,' said the robber, turning upon Heywood, who was sitting at the cashier's desk. 'Open that safe—quick or I'll blow your head off.'

"Pitts then ran to the vault and stepped inside, whereupon Heywood followed him and tried to shut him in.

"One of the robbers seized him and said:

"'Open that safe now or you haven't but a minute to live.'

"'There's a time lock on,' Heywood answered, 'and it can't be opened now.'"

Howard drew a knife from his pocket and made a feint to cut Heywood's throat, as he lay on the floor where he had been thrown in the scuffle, and Pitts told me afterward that Howard fired a pistol near Heywood's head to scare him.

Bunker tried to get a pistol that lay near him, but Pitts saw his movement and beat him to it. It was found on Charley when he was killed, so much more evidence to identify us as the men who were in Northfield.

"Where's the money outside the safe?" Bob asked.

Bunker showed him a box of small change on the counter, and while Bob was putting the money in a grainsack Bunker took advantage of the opportunity to dash out of the rear window. The shutters were closed, and this caused Bunker an instant's delay that was almost fatal. Pitts chased him with a bullet. The first one missed him, but the second went through his right shoulder.

As the men left the bank Heywood clambered to his feet and Pitts, in his liquor, shot him through the head, inflicting the wound that killed him.

We had no time to wreck the telegraph office, and the alarm was soon sent throughout the country.

Gov. John S. Pillsbury first offered $1,000 reward for the arrest of the six who had escaped, and this he changed afterward to $1,000 for each of them, dead or alive. The Northfield bank offered $700 and the Winona & St. Peter railroad $500.

29

A Chase to the Death

A little way out of Northfield we met a farmer and borrowed one of his horses for Pitts to ride. We passed Dundas on the run, before the news of the robbery had reached there, and at Millersburg, too, we were in advance of the news, but at Shieldsville we were behind it. Here a squad of men, who, we afterwards learned, were from Faribault, had left their guns outside a house. We did not permit them to get their weapons until we had watered our horses and got a fresh start. They overtook us about four miles west of Shieldsville, and shots were exchanged without effect on either side. A spent bullet did hit me on the "crazy bone," and as I was leading Bob's horse it caused a little excitement for a minute, but that was all.

We were in a strange country. On the prairie our maps were all right, but when we got into the big woods and among the lakes we were practically lost.

There were a thousand men on our trail, and watching for us at fords and bridges where it was thought we would be apt to go.

That night it started to rain, and we wore out our horses. Friday we moved toward Waterville, and Friday night we camped between Elysian and German lake. Saturday morning we left our horses and started through on foot, hiding that day on an island in a swamp. That night we tramped all night and we spent Sunday about four miles south of Marysburg. Meantime our pursuers were watching for horsemen, not finding our abandoned horses, it seems, until Monday or Tuesday.

Bob's shattered elbow was requiring frequent attention, and

that night we made only nine miles, and Monday, Monday night and Tuesday we spent in a deserted farm-house close to Mankato. That day a man named Dunning discovered us and we took him prisoner. Some of the boys wanted to kill him, on the theory that "dead men tell no tales," while others urged binding him and leaving him in the woods. Finally we administered to him an oath not to betray our whereabouts until we had time to make our escape, and he agreed not to. No sooner, however, was he released than he made posthaste into Mankato to announce our presence, and in a few minutes another posse was looking for us.

Suspecting, however, that he would do so, we were soon on the move, and that night we evaded the guard at the Blue Earth river bridge, and about midnight made our way through Mankato. The whistle on the oil mill blew, and we feared that it was a signal that had been agreed upon to alarm the town in case we were observed, but we were not molested.

Howard and Woods, who had favored killing Dunning, and who felt we were losing valuable time because of Bob's wound, left us that night and went west. As we afterward learned, this was an advantage to us as well as to them, for they stole two horses soon after leaving us, and the posse followed the trail of these horses, not knowing that our party had been divided.

Accordingly, we were not pursued, having kept on a course toward Madelia to a farm where I knew there were some good horses, once in possession of which we could get along faster.

We had been living on scant rations, corn, watermelon and other vegetables principally, but in spite of this Bob's arm was mending somewhat. He had to sleep with it pillowed on my breast, Jim being also crippled with a wound in his shoulder, and we could not get much sleep. The wound in my thigh was troubling me and I had to walk with a cane I cut in the brush. One place we got a chicken and cooked it, only to be interrupted before we could have our feast, having to make a quick dash for cover.

At every stopping place we left marks of blood from our wounds, and could have been easily trailed had not the pursuers been led in the track of our recent companions.

It seems from what I have read since, however, that I had myself left with my landlord at Madelia, Col. Vought, of the Flanders house, a damaging suggestion which proved the ultimate undoing of our party. I had talked with him about a bridge between two lakes near there, and accordingly when it became known that the robbers had passed Mankato Vought thought of this bridge, and it was guarded by him and others for two nights. When they abandoned the guard, however, he admonished a Norwegian boy named Oscar Suborn* to keep close watch there for us, and Thursday morning, Sept. 21, just two weeks after the robbery, Oscar saw us, and fled into town with the alarm. A party of forty was soon out in search for us, headed by Capt. W. W. Murphy, Col. Vought and Sheriff Glispin. They came up with us as we were fording a small slough, and unable to ford it with their horses, they were delayed somewhat by having to go around it. But they soon after got close enough so that one of them broke my walking stick with a shot. We were in sight of our long-sought horses when they cut us off from the animals, and our last hope was gone. We were at bay on the open prairie, surrounded by a picket line of forty men, some of whom would fight. Not prepared to stand for our last fight against such odds on the open field, we fell back into the Watonwan river bottoms and took refuge in some bushes.

We were prepared to wait as long as they would, but they were not of the waiting kind. At least some of them were not, and soon we heard the captain, who, we afterward learned, was W. W. Murphy, calling for volunteers to go in with him and rout us out. Six stepped to the front, Sheriff Glispin, Col. T. L. Vought, B. M. Rice, G. A. Bradford, C. A. Pomeroy and S. J. Severson.

* A pseudonym of Asle Oscar Sorbel, who apparently feared reprisals by gang members and their friends

Forming in line four paces apart, he ordered them to advance rapidly and concentrate the fire of the whole line the instant the robbers were discovered.

Meanwhile we were planning, too.

"Pitts," I said, "if you want to go out and surrender, go on."

"I'll not go," he replied, game to the last. "I can die as well as you can."

"Make for the horses," I said. "Every man for himself. There is no use stopping to pick up a comrade here, for we can't get him through the line. Just charge them and make it if we can."

I got up as the signal for the charge and we fired one volley.

I tried to get my man, and started through, but the next I knew I was lying on the ground, bleeding from my nose and mouth, and Bob was standing up, shouting:

"Coward!"

One of the fellows in the outer line, not brave enough himself to join the volunteers who had come in to beat us out, was not disposed to believe in the surrender, and had his gun levelled on Bob in spite of the handkerchief which was waving as a flag of truce.

Sheriff Glispin, of Watonwan county, who was taking Bob's pistol from him, was also shouting to the fellow:

"Don't shoot him or I'll shoot you."

All of us but Bob had gone down at the first fire. Pitts, shot through the heart, lay dead. Jim, including the wound in the shoulder he received at Northfield, had been shot five times, the most serious being the shot which shattered his upper jaw and lay imbedded beneath the brain, and a shot that buried itself underneath his spine, and which gave him trouble to the day of his death. Including those received in and on the way from Northfield I had eleven wounds.

A bullet had pierced Bob's right lung, but he was the only one left on his feet. His right arm useless, and his pistol empty, he had no choice.

"I surrender," he had shouted. "They're all down but me. Come on. I'll not shoot."

And Sheriff Glispin's order not to shoot was the beginning of the protectorate that Minnesota people established over us.

We were taken into Madelia that day and our wounds dressed, and I greeted my old landlord, Col. Vought, who had been one of the seven to go in to get us. We were taken to his hotel and a guard posted.

Then came the talk of mob vengeance we had heard so often in Missouri. It was said a mob would be out that night to lynch us. Sheriff Glispin swore we would never be mobbed as long as we were his prisoners.

"I don't want any man to risk his life for us," I said to him, "but if they do come for us give us our pistols so we can make a fight for it."

"If they do come, and I weaken," he said, "you can have your pistols."

But the only mob that came was the mob of sightseers, reporters and detectives.

30

To Prison for Life

Saturday we were taken to Faribault, the county seat of Rice county, in which Northfield is, and here there was more talk of lynching, but Sheriff Ara Barton was not of that kind either, and we were guarded by militia until the excitement had subsided. A Faribault policeman, who thought the militia guard was a bluff, bet five dollars he could go right up to the jail without being interfered with. He did not halt when challenged, and was fired upon and killed, the coroner's jury acquitting the militiaman who shot him. Some people blamed us for his death, too.

Chief of Detectives McDonough, of St. Louis, whom I had passed a few months before in the union depot at St. Louis, was among our visitors at Faribault.

Another was Detective Bligh, of Louisville, who believed then, and probably did ever afterward, that I had been in the Huntington, West Virginia, robbery, and tried to pump me about it.

Four indictments were found against us. One charged us with being accessory to the murder of Cashier Heywood, another with assaulting Bunker with intent to do great bodily harm, and the third with robbing the First National bank of Northfield. The fourth charged me as principal and my brothers as accessories with the murder of Gustavson. Two witnesses had testified before the grand jury identifying me as the man who fired the shot that hit him, although I know I did not, because I fired no shot in that part of town.

Although not one of us had fired the shot that killed either Heywood or Gustavson, our attorneys, Thomas Rutledge of Madelia and Bachelder and Buckham of Faribault, asked, when we were arraigned, Nov. 9, that we be given two days in which to plead.

They advised us that as accessories were equally guilty with the principals, under the law, and as by pleading guilty we could escape capital punishment, we should plead guilty. There was little doubt, under the circumstances, of our conviction, and under the law as it stood then, an accused murderer who pleaded guilty was not subject to the death penalty. The state was new, and the law had been made to offer an inducement to murderers not to put the county to the expense of a trial.

The excitement that followed our sentence to state prison, which was popularly called "cheating the gallows," resulted in the change of the law in that respect.

The following Saturday we pleaded guilty, and Judge Lord

sentenced us to imprisonment for the remainder of our lives in the state prison at Stillwater, and a few days later we were taken there by Sheriff Barton.

With Bob it was a life sentence, for he died there of consumption Sept. 16, 1889. He was never strong physically after the shot pierced his lung in the last fight near Madelia.

31

Some Private History

Every blood-and-thunder history of the Younger brothers declares that Frank and Jesse James were the two members of the band that entered Northfield who escaped arrest or death.

They were not, however. One of those two men was killed afterward in Arizona and the other died from fever some years afterward.

There were reasons why the James and the Younger brothers could not take part in any such project as that at Northfield.

Frank James and I came together as soldiers some little time before the Lawrence raid. He was a good soldier, and while he never was higher than a private the distinctions between the officers and the men were not as finely drawn in Quantrill's command as they are nowadays in military life. As far back as 1862, Frank James and I formed a friendship, which has existed to this day.

Jesse James I never met, as I have already related, until the early summer of 1866. The fact that all of us were liable to the visits of posses when least expected gave us one interest in common, the only one we ever did have, although we were thrown together more or less through my friendship with Frank James.

The beginning of my trouble with Jesse came in 1872, when

George W. Shepherd returned to Lee's Summit after serving a term in prison in Kentucky for the bank robbery at Russellville in 1868.

Jesse had told me that Shepherd was gunning for me, and accordingly one night, when Shepherd came late to the home of Silas Hudspeth, where I was, I was prepared for trouble, as in fact, I always was anyway.

When Shepherd called, Hudspeth shut the door again, and told me who was outside. I said "let him in," and stepping to the door with my pistol in my hand, I said:

"Shepherd, I am in here; you're not afraid, are you?"

"That's all right," he answered. "Of course I'm not afraid." The three of us talked till bedtime, when Hudspeth told us to occupy the same bed. I climbed in behind, and as was my custom, took my pistol to bed with me. Shepherd says he did not sleep a wink that night, but I did. At breakfast next morning, I said:

"I heard yesterday that you intended to kill me on sight; have you lost your nerve?"

"Who told you that, Cole?" he answered.

"I met Jess yesterday and he told me that you sent that message to me by him."

Soon after I met Jesse James, and but for the interference of friends we would have shot it out then and there.

My feeling toward Jesse became more bitter in the latter part of that year, when after the gate robbery at the Kansas City fair, he wrote a letter to the Times of that city declaring that he and I had been accused of the robbery, but that he could prove an alibi. So far as I know that is the first time my name was ever mentioned in connection with the Kansas City robbery.

In 1874, when Detective Whicher was killed on a trip to arrest Frank and Jesse James, I was angered to think that Jesse and his friends had brought Whicher from Kearney to the south side of the river, which I then believed was done to throw suspicion on the boys in Jackson county, of whom, perhaps, I would be most likely to get the credit. I have since learned, however, from the men who did kill Whicher, that Jesse did not kill him, but had believed his story and had been inclined to welcome him as a fellow wanderer. Whicher declared that he had murdered his wife and children in the East and he was seeking a refuge from the officers of the law. But Jesse's comrades were skeptical, and when they found on Whicher a pistol bearing Pinkerton's mark, they started with him for Kansas City intending to leave him dead in the street there. Shortly after they crossed to the Independence side of the river, the sound of a wagon on the frozen ground impelled them to finish the job where they were, as it was almost daybreak and they did not want to be seen with their captive.

But Jesse and I were not on friendly terms at any time after the Shepherd affair, and never were associated in any enterprises.

32

Lost—Twenty-five Years

When the iron doors shut behind us at the Stillwater prison I submitted to the prison discipline with the same unquestioning obedience that I had exacted during my military service, and Jim and Bob, I think, did the same.

For ten years and a half after our arrival, Warden Reed remained. The first three years there was a popular idea that such desperate men as the Youngers would not stay long behind prison walls, and that especial watchfulness must be exercised in our case. Accordingly the three of us were put at work making buckets and tubs, with Ben Cayou over us as a special guard, when in our dreams we had been traveling to South America on Ben Butler's money.

Then we were put in the thresher factory. I made the sieves, while Jim sewed the belts, and Bob made the straw-carriers and elevators.

The latter part of the Reed regime I was in the storeroom.

Jan. 25, 1884, when we had been in the prison something over seven years, the main prison building was destroyed by fire at night. George P. Dodd, who was then connected with the prison, while his wife was matron, and who still lives in Buffalo, Minn., said of our behavior that night:

"I was obliged to take the female convicts from their cells and place them in a small room that could not be locked. The Youngers were passing and Cole asked if they could be of any service. I said: 'Yes, Cole. Will you three boys take care of Mrs. Dodd and the women?' Cole answered: 'Yes, we will, and if you ever had any confidence in us place it in us now.' I told him I had the utmost confidence and I slipped a pistol to Cole as I had two. Jim, I think, had an ax handle and Bob a little pinch bar. The boys stood before the door of the little room for hours and even took the blankets they had brought with them from their cells and gave them to the women to try and keep them comfortable as it was very cold. When I could take charge of the women and the boys were relieved, Cole returned my revolver."

Next morning Warden Reed was flooded with telegrams and newspaper sensations: "Keep close watch of the Youngers;" "Did the Youngers escape?" "Plot to free the Youngers," and that sort of thing.

The warden came to his chief deputy, Abe Hall, and suggested that we be put in irons, not that he had any fear on our account, but for the effect on the public.

"I'll not put irons on 'em," replied Hall.

And that day Hall and Judge Butts took us in a sleigh down town to the county jail where we remained three or four weeks. That was the only time we were outside the prison enclosure from 1876 till 1901.

When H. G. Stordock became warden, I was made librarian,

while Jim carried the mail and Bob was clerk to the steward, where we remained during the administration of Wardens Randall and Garvin, except Bob, who wasted away from consumption and died in September, 1889.

When Warden Wolfer came to the prison, he put Jim in charge of the mail and the library, and I was set at work in the laundry temporarily while the new hospital building was being made ready. I was then made head nurse in the hospital, and remained there until the day we were paroled, Warden Reeve, who was there for two years under the administration of Gov. Lind, leaving us there.

Every one of these wardens was our friend, and the deputy wardens, too. Abe Hall, Will Reed, A. D. Westby, Sam A. Langum, T. W. Alexander, and Jack Glennon were all partisans of ours. If any reader misses one name from this list of deputy wardens, there is nothing I have to say for or against him.

Dr. Pratt, who was prison physician when we went to Stillwater, Dr. T. C. Clark, who was his assistant, and Dr. B. J. Merrill, who has been prison physician since, have been staunch partisans of the Younger boys in the efforts of our friends to secure our pardon. And the young doctors with whom I was thrown in close contact during their service as assistant prison physicians, Drs. Sidney Boleyn, Gustavus A. Newman, Dan Beebe, A. E. Hedbeck, Morrill Withrow, and Jenner Chance, have been most earnest in their championship of our cause.

The stewards, too, Benner, and during the Reeve regime, Smithton, which whom as head nurse I was thrown in direct contact, never had any difficulty with me, although Benner with a twinkle in his eye, would say to me:

"Cole, I believe you come and get peaches for your patients up there long after they are dead."

The invalids in that hospital always got the delicacies they wanted, subject to the physician's permission, if what they wanted was to be found anywhere in Stillwater or in St. Paul.

The prison hospital building is not suitable for such use, and a new hospital building is needed, but no fault can be found with the way invalid prisoners are cared for at Stillwater.

When there is added a new hospital building, and the present hospital is transformed into an insane ward, Stillwater will indeed be a model prison.

Words fail me when I seek to express my gratitude to the host of friends who were glad to plead our cause during the later years of our confinement at Stillwater, and especially to Warden Henry Wolfer and his family, every one of whom was a true friend to Jim and myself.

33

The Star of Hope

In spite of the popular indignation our crime had justly caused, from the day the iron gates closed behind us in 1876, there were always friends who hoped and planned for our ultimate release. Some of these were misguided, and did us more harm than good.

Among these were two former guerrillas, who committed small crimes that they might be sent to prison and there plot with us for our escape. One of them was only sent to the county jail, and the other served a year in Stillwater prison without ever seeing us.

Well meaning, too, but unfortunate, was the declaration of Missouri friends in Minnesota that they could raise $100,000 to get us out of Stillwater.

But as the years went by, the popular feeling against us not only subsided, but our absolute submission to the minutest details of prison discipline won for us the consideration, I might even say the high esteem of the prison officials who came in contact with us, and as the Northfield tragedy became more and more remote, those who favored out pardon became more numerous, and yearly numbered in their ranks more and more of the influential people of the state, who believed that our crime had been avenged, and that Jim and I, the only survivors of the tragedy, would be worthy citizens if restored to freedom.

My Missouri friends are surprised to find that I prize friendships in Minnesota, a state where I found so much trouble, but in spite of Northfield, and all its tragic memories, I have in Minnesota some of the best friends a man ever had on earth.

Every governor of Minnesota from as early as 1889 down to 1899 was petitioned for our pardon, but not one of them was satisfied of the advisability of a full pardon, and the parole system provided by the enlightened humanitarianism of the state for other convicts did not apply to lifers.

Under this system a convict whose prison record is good may be paroled on his good behavior after serving half of the term for which he was sentenced.

The reiterated requests for our pardon, coming from men the governors had confidence in, urging them to a pardon they were reluctant to grant, led to a feeling, which found expression finally in official circles, that the responsibility of the pardoning power should be divided by the creation of a board of pardons as existed in some other states.

It was at first proposed that the board should consist of the governor, attorney general and the warden of the prison, but before the bill passed, Senator Allen J. Greer secured the substitution for the chief justice for the warden, boasting, when the amendment was made:

"That ties the Youngers up for as long as Chief Justice Start lives."

A unanimous vote of the board was required to grant a pardon, and as Chief Justice Start had lived in the vicinity of Northfield at the time of the raid in 1876, many people believed that he would never consent to our pardon.

In the legislature of 1889, our friends endeavored to have the parole system extended to life prisoners, and secured the introduction in the legislature of a bill to provide that life prisoners might be paroled when they had served such a period as would have entitled them to their release had they been sentenced to imprisonment for 35 years. The bill was drawn by George M. Bennett of Minneapolis, who had taken a great deal of interest in our case, and was introduced in the senate by Senator George P. Wilson, of Minneapolis. As the good time allowances on a 35-year sentence would cut it to between 23 and 24 years, we could have been paroled in a few months had this bill passed. Although there was one other inmate of the prison who might have come under its provisions, it was generally known as the "Youngers' parole bill" and the feeling against it was largely identified with the feeling against us. I am told, however, since my release, that it would have passed at that session had it not been for the cry of "money" that was used. There never was a dollar used in Minnesota to secure our pardon, and before our release we had some of the best men and women in the state working in our behalf, without money and without price. But this outcry defeated the bill of 1899.

Still it did not discourage our friends on the outside.

At the next session of the legislature, 1901, there was finally passed the bill which permitted our conditional parole, the pardon board not being ready to grant us our full freedom. This bill provided for the parole of any life convict who had been confined for twenty years, on the unanimous consent of the board of pardons.

The bill was introduced in the house by Representative P. C. Deming of Minneapolis, and among those who worked for its passage was Representative Jay W. Phillips, who, as a boy, had been driven from the streets the day we entered Northfield. Senator Wilson, who had introduced the bill which failed in 1899, was again a staunch supporter and led the fight for us in the senate.

The board of prison managers promptly granted the parole, the principal conditions of which were as follows:

"He shall not exhibit himself in any dime museum, circus, theater, opera house, or any other place of public amusement or assembly where a charge is made for admission.

"He shall on the twentieth day of each month write the warden of the state prison a report of himself, stating whether he had been constantly at work during the last month, and if not, why not; how much he has earned, and how much he has expended, together with a general statement as to his surroundings and prospects, which must be indorsed by his employer.

"He shall in all respects conduct himself honestly, avoid evil associations, obey the law, and abstain from the use of intoxicating liquors.

"He shall not go outside the state of Minnesota."

The parole was unanimously concurred in by Messrs. B. F. Nelson, F. W. Temple, A. C. Weiss, E. W. Wing, and R. H. Bronson, of the prison board and urged by Warden Henry Wolfer.

The board of pardons, in indorsing our parole, said:

"We are satisfied that the petitioners in this case have by exceptionally good conduct in prison for a quarter of a century, and the evidence they have given of sincere reformation, earned the right to a parole, if any life prisoner can do so."

And July 14, 1901, Jim and I went out into the world for the first time in within a few months of twenty-five years.

Rip Van Winkle himself was not so long away. St. Paul and Minneapolis which, when we were there in 1876, had less than 75,000 people all told, had grown to cities within whose limits were over 350,000. A dozen railroads ended in one or the other of these centers of business that we had known as little better than frontier towns.

34

On Parole

Our first positions after our release from prison were in the employ of the P. N. Peterson Granite company, of St. Paul and Stillwater, Mr. Peterson having known us since early in our prison life.*

We were to receive $60 a month each and expenses. Jim was to take care of some office work, and take orders in the immediate vicinity of Stillwater. He worked mostly through Washington county, and with a horse and buggy, but had not been at work more than two months when the sudden starting of the horse as he was getting out of the buggy started anew his intermittent trouble with the bullet that lodged under his spine, and he was compelled to find other employment.

He then went into the cigar department of the Andrew Schoch grocery company in St. Paul, and after several months there was employed by Maj. Elwin, of the Elwin cigar company in Minneapolis, where he remained until a few days before his death.

I traveled for the Peterson company until Nov., 1901, covering nearly all of Minnesota. But the change from the regularity of prison hours to the irregular hours, meals and various changes to which the drummer is subject was too much for me, and I returned to St. Paul to enter the employ of Edward J. and Hubert C. Schurmeier, who had been strenuous workers for my pardon,

---

* The Peterson company specialized in monuments and tombstones.

and James Nugent at the Interstate institute for the cure of the liquor and morphine habits, on Rosabel street in St. Paul.*

There I remained several months, and then was employed by John J. O'Connor, chief of police at St. Paul, in connection with private interests to which he could not give his personal attention.

35

Jim Gives It Up

The bullet wound which Jim received in our last fight near Madelia, shattering his upper jaw, and remaining imbedded near his brain, until it was removed by Dr. T. C. Clark after we were in the prison at Stillwater, affected Jim at intervals during all his prison life, and he would have periodical spells of depression, during which he would give up all hope, and his gloomy spirits would repel the sympathy of those who were disposed to cheer him up.

I remember that at the time of the fire in 1884, he was in one of these fits of depression, but the excitement of that time buoyed him up, and he was himself again for a considerable period.

After our release from prison, Jim's precarious health and his inability to rejoin his family in Missouri combined to make these fits of depression more frequent. While he was working for Maj. Elwin, instead of putting in his afternoons, which were free, among men, or enjoying the sunshine and air which had so long been out of our reach, he would go to his room and revel in socialistic literature, which only tended to overload a mind already

* Edward J. Schurmeier was secretary and treasurer of the J. H. Schurmeier Wagon & Carriage Co.; Hubert C. Schurmeier was president of the Inter-State Institute.

surcharged with troubles. For my part, I tried to get into the world again, to live down the past, and I could and did enjoy the theaters, although Jim declared he would never set foot in one until he could go a free man. In July, he and some of his friends petitioned the board of pardons for a full pardon, but the board was of the opinion that it was too early to consider that, believing that we should be kept on our good behavior for a time.

That resulted in another fit of depression for Jim. He took it to heart, and never regained his cheerful mood, for when he was up, he was away up, and when down, away down. There was no half way place with Jim.

In October, 1902, he left Maj. Elwin expecting to go to St. Paul to work for Yerxa Bros.

But Sunday afternoon, Oct. 19, his dead body was found in a room at the hotel Reardon, Seventh and Minnesota streets, St. Paul, where he had been staying since leaving Minneapolis. His trunk had been sent to friends, and there was every indication that he had carefully planned his death by his own hand. A bullet hole above his right ear and a pistol clutched in his hand, told the story of suicide. Dr. J. M. Finnell, who as acting coroner, was summoned, decided that he must have shot himself early in the forenoon, although neighbors in the block had not been disturbed by the shot.

I was sick in bed at the time and my physician, Dr. J. J. Platt, forbade my attempting to do anything in the premises, but Jim's body was taken in charge in my behalf by Chief of Police O'Connor, and borne to Lee's Summit, Mo., our old Jackson county home, where it was laid to rest.

The pallbearers were C. W. Wigginton, O. H. Lewis, H. H. McDowell, Sim Whitsett, William Gregg and William Lewis, all old neighbors or comrades during the war.

Some people obtained the idea that it was Jim's wish that he be cremated, but this idea grew out of a letter he left showing his gloomy condition. It "roasted" Gov. Van Sant and Warden Wolfer and the board of pardons, declared for socialism, and urged Bryan to come out for it.

On the outside of the envelope was written:

"All relations stay away from me. No crocodile tears wanted. Reporters, be my friends. Burn me up.—Jim Younger."

I think the "burn me up" was an admonition to the reporters. Jim always felt that the papers had been bitter to us, although some of them had been staunch supporters of the proposal for our parole. The day we were paroled, Jim said to a visiting newspaper woman:

"When we get out we would like to be left in peace. We don't want to be stared at and we don't want to be interviewed. For twenty-five years now, we have been summoned here to have men stare at us and question us and then go back and write up what they think and believe. It's hard to have people write things about you that are not true and put words in your mouth that you never uttered."

It was to such newspaper men, I think, that Jim sent his message "Burn me up."

36

Free Again

Jim's tragic death brought the Youngers again into the public eye, and aside from any effort on my part, there was a renewed discussion of the advisability of extending a full pardon to me, the lone survivor of the band who had invaded Northfield.

At the next quarterly meeting of the board, which was held in January of this year, the matter was taken up, and the board considered my application, which was for an absolute or a conditional pardon as the board might see fit.

It was urged on my behalf that the limitation clause confining me to Minnesota was one that it might be well to do away with, as it prevented me from joining my friends and relatives in Missouri, and kept me in a state, where a great many people did not really care for my society, although so many were very kind and cordial to me.

Against this it was urged that while I was in the state, the board could exercise a supervision of my employment and movements which it might be judicious to continue.

After carefully considering the various arguments for and against my absolute pardon, the board decided against it, but at a special meeting held February 4, 1903, voted unanimously for a conditional pardon as follows:

"Having carefully considered this matter, with a keen appreciation of our duty to the public and to the petitioner, we have reached the conclusion that his conduct for twenty-five years in prison, and his subsequent conduct as a paroled prisoner, justify the belief that if his request to be permitted to return to his friends and kindred be granted, he will live and remain at liberty without any violation of the law.

"We are, however, of the opinion that his absolute pardon would not be compatible with the welfare of this state—the scene of his crime—for the reason that his presence therein, if freed from the conditions of his parole, would create a morbid and demoralizing interest in him and his crime.

"Therefore it is ordered that a pardon be granted to Thomas Coleman Younger, upon the condition precedent and subsequent that he return without unnecessary delay to his friends and kindred whence he came, and that he never voluntarily come back to Minnesota.

"And upon the further condition that he file with the governor of the State of Minnesota his written promise that he will never exhibit himself or allow himself to be exhibited, as an actor or participant in any public performance, museum, circus, theater, opera house or any other place of public amusement or assembly where a charge is made for admission; Provided, that this shall not exclude him from attending any such public performance or place of amusement.

"If he violates any of the conditions of this pardon, it shall be absolutely void.

S. R. Van Sant, Governor.

Chas. M. Start, Chief Justice of the Supreme Court

Wallace B. Douglas, Attorney-General."

A few days later I filed with Governor Van Sant the following:

"I, Thomas Coleman Younger, pursuant to one of the conditions upon which a pardon has been granted to me, do hereby promise upon my honor that I will never exhibit myself, nor allow myself to be exhibited, as an actor or participant in any public performance, museum, circus, theater, opera house, or any place of public amusement or assembly where a charge is made for admission."

37

The Wild West

The "Cole Younger and Frank James' Historical Wild West Show" is an effort on the part of two men whose exploits have been more wildly exaggerated, perhaps, than those of any other men living, to make an honest living and demonstrate to the people of America that they are not as black as they have been painted.

There will be nothing in the Wild West show to which any exception can be taken, and it is my purpose, as a part owner in the show, and I have put in the contracts with my partners, that no crookedness nor rowdyism will be permitted by attaches of the show. We will assist the local authorities, too, in ridding the show of the sort of camp-followers who frequently make traveling shows the scapegoat for their misdoings. We propose to have our show efficiently and honestly policed, to give the people the worth of their money, and to give an entertainment that will show the frontiersman of my early manhood as he was.

I had hoped if my pardon had been made unconditional, to earn a livelihood on the lecture platform. I had prepared a lecture which I do think would not have harmed any one, while it might have impressed a valuable lesson on those who took it to heart.

I give it herewith under the title, "What My Life Has Taught Me."

38

What My Life Has Taught Me

Looking back through the dimly lighted corridors of the past, down the long vista of time, a time when I feared not the face of mortal man, nor battalions of men, when backed by my old comrades in arms, it may seem inconsistent to say that I appear before you with a timidity born of cowardice, but perhaps you will understand better than I can tell you that twenty-five years in a prison cell fetters a man's intellect as well as his body. Therefore I disclaim any pretensions to literary merit, and trust that my sincerity of purpose will compensate for my lack of eloquence; and, too, I am not so sure that I care for that kind of oratory that leaves the points to guess at, but rather the simple language of the soul that needs no interpreter.

Let me say, ladies and gentlemen, that the farthest thought

from my mind is that of posing as a character. I do not desire to stand upon the basis of the notoriety which the past record of my life may have earned for me.

Those of you who have been drawn here by mere curiosity to see a character or a man, who by the events of his life has gained somewhat of notoriety, will miss the real object of this lecture and the occasion which brings us together. My soul's desire is to benefit you by recounting some of the important lessons which my life has taught me.

Life is too short to make any other use of it. Besides, I owe too much to my fellow men, to my opportunities, to my country, to my God and to myself, to make any other use of the present occasion.

Since I am to speak to you of some of the important lessons of my life, it may be in order to give you some account of my ancestry. It is something to one's credit to have had an ancestry that one need not be ashamed of. One of the poets said, while talking to a select party of aristocracy:

> "Depend upon it, my snobbish friend,
> Your family line you can't ascend
> Without good reason to apprehend
> You'll find it waxed at the farther end
> With some plebeian vocation;
> Or, what is worse, your family line
> May end in a loop of stronger twine
> That plagued some worthy relation."

But I am proud to say, ladies and gentlemen, that no loop of stronger twine that he referred to ever plagued any relation of mine. No member of our family or ancestry was ever punished for any crime or infringement of the law. My father was a direct descendant from the Lees on one side and the Youngers on the other. The Lees came from Scotland tracing their line back to Bruce. The Youngers were from the city of Strasburg on the

Rhine, descending from the ruling family of Strasburg when that was a free city.

My sainted mother was a direct descendant from the Sullivans, Ladens and Percivals of South Carolina, the Taylors of Virginia, and the Fristoes of Tennessee. Richard Fristoe, mother's father, was one of three judges appointed by the governor of Missouri to organize Jackson county, and was then elected one of the first members of the legislature. Jackson county was so named in honor of his old general, Andrew Jackson, with whom he served at the battle of New Orleans.

My father and mother were married at Independence, the county seat of Jackson county, and there they spent many happy years, and there my own happy childhood days were spent. There were fourteen children of us; I was the seventh. There were seven younger than myself. How often in the dark days of the journey over the sea of life have I called up the happy surroundings of my early days when I had a noble father and dear mother to appeal to in faith for counsel. There had never been a death in the family up to 1860, except among our plantation negroes. Mine was a happy childhood.

I do not desire to pose as an instructor for other people, yet one man's experience may be of value to another, and it may not be presumptuous for me to tell some of the results of experience, a teacher whose lessons are severe, but, at least, worthy of consideration. I might say, perhaps, with Shakespeare, "I have bought golden opinions from all sorts of people."

The subject of my discourse tonight is the index of what is to follow.

I believe that no living man can speak upon his theme with more familiarity. I have lived the gentleman, the soldier, the outlaw, and the convict, living the best twenty-five years of my life in a felon's cell. I have no desire to pose as a martyr, for men who sin must suffer, but I will punctuate my remarks with bold statements, for the eagle should not be afraid of the storm.

It is said that there are but three ways by which we arrive at knowledge in this world; by instruction, by observation, and by experience. We must learn our lessons in life by some one or all of these methods. Those of us who do not, or will not, learn by instruction or by observation are necessarily limited to the fruits of experience. The boy who is told by his mother that fire burns, and who has seen his brother badly burned, surely does not need to have the fact still more clearly impressed upon his mind by experience. Yet in the majority of cases, it takes experience to satisfy him. By a kind of necessity which I cannot at this point stop to explain, I have had to learn some very impressive lessons of my life by the stern teacher, experience. Some people express a desire to live life over again, under the impression that they could make a better success of it on a second trip; such people are scarcely logical—however sincere they may be in a wish of this kind. They seem to forget that by the unfailing law of cause and effect, were they to go back on the trail to the point from which they started and try it over again, under the same circumstances they would land about where they are now. The same causes would produce the same effect.

I confess that I have no inexpressible yearnings to try my life over again, even if it were possible to do so. I have followed the trail of my life for something over fifty years. It has led me into varied and strange experiences.

The last twenty-six years, by a train of circumstances I was not able to control, brought me to the present place and hour. Perhaps it may be proper for me to say, with St. Peter, on the mount of transfiguration, it is good to be here.

The man who chooses the career of outlawry is either a natural fool or an innocent madman. The term outlaw has a varied meaning. A man may be an outlaw, and yet a patriot. There is the outlaw with a heart of velvet and a hand of steel; there is the outlaw who never molested the sacred sanctity of any man's home; there is the outlaw who never dethroned a woman's honor, or assailed her heritage; and there is the outlaw who has never robbed the honest poor. Have you heard of the outlaw who, in the far-off Western land, where the sun dips to the horizon in infinite beauty, was the adopted son of the Kootenai Indians? It was one of the saddest scenes in all the annals of human tragedy. It was during one of those fierce conflicts which characterized earlier frontier days.

The white outlaw had influenced the red man to send a message of peace to the whites, and for this important mission the little son of the Kootenai chief was selected. The young fawn mounted his horse, but before the passport of peace was delivered the brave little courier was shot to pieces by a cavalcade of armed men who slew him before questioning his mission. The little boy was being stripped of the adornments peculiar to Indians when the outlaw rode upon the scene.

"Take your hands off him, or by the God, I'll cut them off," he shouted. "You have killed a lone child—the messenger of peace—peace which I risked my life to secure for the white men who outlawed me."

Taking the dead body tenderly in his arms, he rode back to face the fury of a wronged people. He understood the penalty but went to offer himself as a ransom, and was shot to death. This, however, is not the class of outlaws I would discuss, for very often force of circumstances makes outlaws of men, but I would speak of the criminal outlaw whom I would spare not nor excuse.

My friends, civilization may be a thin veneer, and the world today may be slimy with hypocrisy, but no man is justified in killing lions to feed dogs.

Outlawry is often a fit companion for treason and anarchy, for which the lowest seats of hell should be reserved. The outlaw, like the commercial freebooter, is often a deformity on the face of nature that darkens the light of God's day.

I need not explain my career as an outlaw, a career that has been gorgeously colored with fiction. To me the word outlaw is a living coal of fire. The past is a tragedy—a tragedy wherein danger lurks in every trail. I may be pardoned for hurrying over a few wild, relentless years that led up to a career of outlawry—a memory that cuts like the sword blades of a squadron of cavalry. The outlaw is like a big black bird, from which every passerby feels licensed to pluck a handful of feathers.

My young friend, if you are endowed with physical strength, valor, and a steady hand, let me warn you to use them well, for the God who gave them is the final victor.

Think of a man born of splendid parents, good surroundings, the best of advantages, a fair intellectuality, with the possibility of being president of the United States, and with courage of a field general. Think of him lying stagnant in a prison cell. This does not apply alone to the highway outlaw, but to those outlaws who are sometimes called by the softer name "financier." Not long ago I heard a man speak of a certain banker, and I was reminded that prisons do not contain all the bad men. He said: "Every dog that dies has some friend to shed a tear, but when that man dies there will be universal rejoicing."

I am not exactly a lead man, but it may surprise you to know that I have been shot between twenty and thirty times and am now carrying over a dozen bullets which have never been extracted. How proud I should have been had I been scarred battling for the honor and glory of my country. Those wounds I received while wearing the gray, I've ever been proud of, and my regret is that I did not receive the rest of them during the war with Spain, for the freedom of Cuba and the honor and glory of this great and glorious republic. But, alas, they were not, and it is a memory embalmed that nails a man to the cross.

I was in prison when the war with Cuba was inaugurated, a war that will never pass from memory while hearts beat responsive to the glory of battle in the cause of humanity. How men turned from the path of peace, and seizing the sword, followed the flag! As the blue ranks of American soldiery scaled the heights of heroism, and the smoke rose from the hot altars of the battle gods and freedom's wrongs avenged, so the memory of Cuba's independence will go down in history, glorious as our own revolution—'76 and '98—twin jewels set in the crown of sister centuries. Spain and the world have learned that beneath the folds of our nation's flag there lurks a power as irresistible as the wrath of God.

Sleep on, side by side in the dim vaults of eternity, Manila Bay and Bunker Hill, Lexington and Santiago, Ticonderoga and San Juan, glorious rounds in Columbia's ladder of fame, growing colossal as the ages roll. Yes, I was in prison than, and let me tell you, dear friends, I do not hesitate to say that God permits few men to suffer as I did, when I awoke to the full realization that I was wearing the stripes instead of a uniform of my country.

Remember, friends, I do not uphold war for commercial pillage. War is a terrible thing, and leads men sometimes out of the common avenues of life. Without reference to myself, men of this land, let me tell you emphatically, dispassionately, and absolutely that war makes savages of men, and dethrones them from reason. It is too often sugarcoated with the word "patriotism" to make it bearable and men call it "National honor."

Come with me to the prison, where for a quarter of a century I have occupied a lonely cell. When the door swings in on you there, the world does not hear your muffled wail. There is little to inspire mirth in prison. For a man who has lived close to the heart of nature, in the forest, in the saddle, to imprison him is like caging a wild bird. And yet imprisonment has brought out the excellencies of many men. I have learned many things in the lonely hours there. I have learned that hope is a divinity; I have learned that a surplus of determination conquers every weakness; I have learned that you cannot mate a white dove to a blackbird; I have learned that vengeance is for God and not for man; I have learned that there are some things better than a picture on a church window; I have learned that the American peo-

ple, and especially the good people of Minnesota, do not strip a
fallen foe; I have learned that whoever says "there is no God" is
a fool; I have learned that politics is often mere traffic, and
statesmanship trickery; I have learned that the honor of the republic is put upon the plains and battled for; I have learned that
the English language is too often used to deceive the common-
wealth of labor; I have learned that the man who prides himself
on getting on the wrong side of every public issue is as pernicious
an enemy to the country as the man who openly fires upon the
flag; and I have seen mute sufferings of men in prison which no
human pen can portray.

And I have seen men die there. During my twenty-five years
of imprisonment, I have spent a large portion of the time in the
hospital, nursing the sick and soothing the dying. Oh! the sad-
ness, the despair, the volcano of human woe that lurks in such
an hour. One, a soldier from the North, I met in battle when I
wore the gray. In '63 I had led him to safety beyond the Confederate lines in Missouri, and in '97 he died in my arms in the Minnesota prison, a few moments before a full pardon had arrived
from the president.

The details of this remarkable coincidence were pathetic in
the extreme, equalled only by the death of my young brother
Bob.

And yet, my dear friends, prisons and prison discipline,
which sometimes destroy the reason, and perpetuate a stigma
upon those who survive them, — these, I say, are the safeguards
of the nation.

A man has plenty of time to think in prison, and I might add
that it is an ideal place for a man to study law, religion, and
Shakespeare, not forgetting the president's messages. However,
I would advise you not to try to get into prison just to find an
ideal place for these particular studies. I find, after careful study,
that law is simply an interpretation of the Ten Commandments,
nothing more, nothing less. All law is founded upon Scripture,

and Scripture, in form of religion or law, rules the universe.

The infidel who ridicules religion is forced to respect the law, which in reality is religion itself.

It is not sufficient alone to make good and just laws, but our people must be educated, or should be, from the cradle up, to respect the law. This is one great lesson to be impressed upon the American people. Let the world know that we are a law-loving nation, for our law is our life.

Experience has taught me that there is no true liberty apart from law. Law is a boundary line, a wall of protection, circumscribing the field in which liberty may have her freest exercise. Beyond the boundary line, freedom must surrender her rights, and change her name to "penalty for transgression." The law is no enemy, but the friend of liberty. The world and the planets move by law. Disregarding the law by which they move, they would become wanderers in the bleak darkness forever.

The human mind in its normal condition moves and works by law. When self-will, blinded by passion or lust, enters her realm, and breaks her protecting laws, mind then loses her sweet liberty of action, and becomes a transgressor. Chaos usurps the throne of liberty, and mind becomes at enmity with law. How many, many times the words of the poet have sung to my soul during the past twenty-six years:

> "Eternal spirit of the chainless mind,
>   Brightest in dungeon's liberty thou art,
>   For there thy habitation is the heart,
>   The heart, which love of thee alone can bind."

Your locomotive with her following load of life and treasure is safe while she keeps the rails, but, suppose that with an insane desire for a larger liberty, she left the rails and struck out for herself a new pathway, ruin, chaos and death would strew her course. And again let me impress the fact upon you. Law is one of humanity's valiant friends. It is the safeguard of the highest personal and national liberties. The French revolution furnishes a standing illustration of society without law.

There are times when I think the American people are not patriotic enough. Some think patriotism is necessary only in time of war, but I say to you it is more necessary in time of peace.

When the safety of the country is threatened, and the flag insulted, we are urged on by national pride to repel the enemy, but in time of peace selfish interests take the greater hold of us, and retard us in our duty to country.

Nowhere is patriotism needed more than at the ballot-box. There the two great contestants are country and self, and unless the spirit of patriotism guides the vote our country is sure to lose. To be faithful citizens we must be honest in our politics. The political star which guides us should be love for our country and our country's laws.

Patriotism, side by side with Christianity, I would have to go down to future generations, for wherever the church is destroyed you are making room for asylums and prisons. With the martyred Garfield, I, too, believe that our great national danger is not from without.

It may be presumptuous in me to proffer so many suggestions to you who have been living in a world from which I have been exiled for twenty-five years. I may have formed a wrong conception of some things, but you will be charitable enough to forgive my errors.

I hope to be of some assistance to mankind and will dedicate my future life to unmask every wrong in my power and aid civilization to rise against further persecution. I want to be the drum-major of a peace brigade, who would rather have the good will of his fellow creatures than shoulder straps from any corporate power.

One of the lessons impressed upon me by my life experience is the power of that which we call personal influence, the power of one mind or character over another.

Society is an aggregate of units. The units are related. No one lives or acts alone, independently of another. Personal influence plays its part in the relations we sustain to each other.

Do you ask me to define what I mean by personal influence? It is the sum total of what a man is, and its effect upon another. Some one has said, "Every man is what God made him," and some are considerably more so. That which we call character is the sum total of all his tendencies, habits, appetite and passions. The terms character and reputation are too often confused. Character is what you really are; reputation is what some one else would have you.

Every man has something of good in him. Probably none of us can say that we are all goodness.

I have noticed that when a man claims to be all goodness, that claim alone does not make his credit any better in business, or at the bank. If a man is good, the world has a way of finding out his qualities. Most men are willing to admit, at least to themselves, that their qualities are somewhat mixed. I do not believe that the good people of the world are all bunched up in one corner and the bad ones in another. Christ's parable of the wheat and the tares explains that to my satisfaction. There is goodness in all men, and sermons even in stones. But goodness and badness is apt to run in streaks. Man, to use the language of another, is a queer combination of cheek and perversity, insolence, pride, impudence, vanity, jealousy, hate, scorn, baseness, insanity, honor, truth, wisdom, virtue and urbanity. He's a queer combination all right. And those mixed elements of his nature, in their effects on other people, we call personal influence. Many a man is not altogether what he has made himself, but what others have made him. But a man's personal influence is within his own control. It is at the gateway of his nature from which his influence goes forth that he needs to post his sentinels.

Mind stands related to mind, somewhat in the relation of cause and effect.

Emerson said, "You send your boy to school to be educated, but the education that he gets is largely from the other boys." It is a kind of education that he will remember longer and have a greater influence upon his character and career in life than the instructions he gets from the teacher.

The great scholar, Elihu Burritt, has said, "No human being can come into this world without increasing or diminishing the sum total of human happiness." No one can detach himself from the connection. There is no spot in the universe to which he can retreat from his relations to others.

This makes living and acting among our fellows a serious business. It makes life a stage, ourselves the actors—some of us being remarkably bad actors—and imposes upon us the obligation to act well our part. Therein all honor lies. And in order to do this it behooves us to stock up with the qualities of mind and character, the influence of which will be helpful to those who follow the trail behind us.

Another plain duty my experience has pointed out is that each of us owes an honest, manly effort toward the material world's progress. Honest labor is the key that unlocks the door of happiness. One of the silliest notions that a young man can get into his head is the idea that the world owes him a living. It does not owe you the fraction of a red cent, young man. What have you done for the world that put it under obligation to you? When did the world become indebted to you? Who cared for you in the years of helpless infancy? Who built the schoolhouse where you got the rudiments of your education? The world was made and equipped for men to develop it. Almighty God furnished the world well. He provided abundant coal beds, oceans of oil, boundless forests, seas of salt. He has ribbed the mountain with gems fit to deck the brows of science, eloquence and art. He has furnished earth to produce for all the requirements of man. He has provided man himself with an intellect to fathom and develop the mysteries of His handiwork. Now He commands that mortal man shall do the rest, and what a generous command it is! And this is the world that owes you a living, is it?

This reminds me of a man who built and thoroughly equipped a beautiful church, and presented it as a gift to the congregation. After expressing their gratitude, a leading member of the church said to the generous donor: "And now may we request that you put a lightning-rod on the church to secure it against lightning?" The giver replied: "No. I have built a church wherein to worship Almighty God, and if He sees fit to destroy it by lightning, let Him strike."

There was a church struck by lightning in New Jersey, where the big trust magnates met for worship, and the Lord is excused for visiting it with lightning. No, the Lord is not going to strike down your good works at all. He has laid out an earthly Paradise for each of us, and nothing is due us except what we earn by honest toil and noble endeavor. We owe the world a debt of gratitude we can never repay for making this a convenient dwelling-place. We owe the world the best there is in us for its development. Gerald Massey put it right when he said: "Toil is creation's crown, worship is duty."

Another important lesson life has taught me is the value, the priceless value, of good friends, and with Shakespeare I say: "Grapple them to thy soul with hooks of steel." Some sage has said: "A man is known by the company he can not get into." But truly this would be a barren world without the association of friends. But a man must make himself worthy of friends, for the text teaches us that "A man who wants friends must show himself friendly." What I am today, or strive to be, I owe largely to my friends—friends to whom I fail in language to express my gratitude, which is deeper than the lips; friends who led us to believe that "stone walls do not a prison make, nor iron bars a cage;" friends who understand that human nature and sincerity are often clothed in prison garb; friends who have decreed that one false step does not lame a man for life.

Oh, what a generous doctrine! And, although unwritten, I believe God has set his seal upon it. Honest friendship is a grand religion, and if we are true to ourselves, the poet tells us, we cannot be false to any man.

However, I am forced to admit that there are many brands of friendship existing these days which had not birth in our time. For instance: A number of men have visited me in the prison, and assured me of their interest in a pardon, etc. They have talked so eloquently and earnestly that I thought I was fortunate to enlist the sympathies and aid of such splendid men. After the first or second visit I was informed as gently as possible that a price was attached to this friendship; how much would I give them for indorsing or signing a petition for a pardon? I remember how I glared at them, how my pulse almost ceased beating, at such demands. What injustice to the public to petition a man out of prison for a price! If a man can not come out of prison on his merits, let him remain there. I hold, too, that if there is honor among thieves there should be among politicians and pretentious citizens. I hate a liar and a false man. I hate a hypocrite, a man whose word to his friend is not as good as gold.

My friends, there is just one thing I will say in my own defense if you will so far indulge me. I do not believe in doing under the cover of darkness that which will not bear the light of day. During my career of outlawing I rode into town under the glare of the noonday sun, and all men knew my mission. Corporations of every color had just cause to despise me then. But no man can accuse me of prowling about at night, nor of ever having robbed an individual, or the honest poor. In our time a man's word was equal to his oath, and seldom did a man break faith when he had once pledged himself to another.

What I say to you, fellow citizens, I say not in idle boast, but from the soul of a man who reverences truth in all its simplicity. Think of it—a price for a man's proffered friendship. On my soul, I do not even now comprehend so monstrous a proposition, and, believe me, even the unfortunate creatures about me in prison looked more like men than your respectable citizens and professional men with a price for their friendship.

I should like to say something to the ladies who have honored me with their presence. But as I have been a bachelor all my life I scarcely know what to say. I do know, though, that they are the divine creatures of a divine Creator; I do know that they are the high priestesses of this land; and, too, I say, God could not be everywhere, so He made woman. One almost needs the lantern of a Diogenes in this progressive age to find an honest man, but not so with a good woman, who is an illumination in herself, the light of her influence shining with a radiance of its own. You will agree with me that the following lines contain more truth than poetry, and I bow to the splendid genius of the author:

"Blame woman not if some appear
   Too cold at times, and some too gay and light;
Some griefs gnaw deep—some woes are hard to bear.
   Who knows the past, and who can judge them right?"

Perhaps you have heard of banquets "for gentlemen only." Well, it was upon one of these occasions that one of the guests was called upon to respond to a toast—"The Ladies."

There being no ladies present, he felt safe in his remarks. "I do not believe," he said, "that there are any real, true women living any more." The guest opposite him sprang to his feet and shouted: "I hope that the speaker refers only to his own female relations." I never could understand, either, when a man goes wrong it is called "misfortune," while if a woman goes wrong it is called "shame." But I presume, being in prison twenty-five years, I am naturally dull, and should not question a world I have not lived in for a quarter of a century. I tell you, my friends, that I know very little of women, but of one thing I am morally certain: If the front seats of Paradise are not reserved for women, I am willing to take a back seat with them. It seems to me that every man who had a mother should have a proper regard for woman-hood. My own mother was a combination of all the best elements of the high character that belong to true wife and mother hood. Her devotion and friendship were as eternal as the very stars of heaven, and no misfortune could dwarf her generous impulses or curdle the milk of human kindness in her good heart. Her memory has been an altar, a guiding star, a divinity, in the darkest hour when regrets were my constant companions. It is true that I was a mere boy, in my teens, when the war was on, but there is no excuse for neglecting a good mother's counsel, and no good can possibly result. I was taught that honor among men and charity in the errors of others were the chief duties of mankind, the fundamentals of law, both human and divine. In those two commandments I have not failed, but in other respects I fell short of my home influence, and so, my young friends, do not do as I have done, but do as I tell you to do—honor the fourth commandment.

There is no heroism in outlawry, and the fate of each outlaw in his turn should be an everlasting lesson to the young of the land. And even as Benedict Arnold, the patriot and traitor, dying in an ugly garret in a foreign land, cried with his last breath to the lone priest beside him: "Wrap my body in the American flag;" so the outlaw, from his inner soul, if not from his lips, cries out, "Oh, God, turn back the universe!"

There is another subject I want to say a word about—one which I never publicly advocated while in prison, for the reason that I feared the outside world would believe it a disguise to obtain my freedom. Freedom is the birthright heritage of every man, and it was very dear to me, but if the price of it was to pretend to be religious, the price was too high, and I would rather have remained in prison. Some men in prison fly to it as a refuge in sincerity—some otherwise. But to the sincere it is a great consolation, for it teaches men that hope is a divinity, without which no man can live and retain his reason.

But now that I have been restored to citizenship I feel free to express my views upon religion without fear that men will accuse me of hypocrisy. I do not see why that word "hypocrisy" was ever put in the English language. Now, I am a lecturer, not a minister, but I want to say that I think it is a wise plan to let the Lord have his own way with you. That's logic. The man who walks with God is in good company. Get into partnership with Him, but don't try to be the leading member of the firm. He knows more about the business than you do. You may be able for a time to practice deception upon your fellow men, but don't try to fire any blank cartridges at the Author of this Universe. There are a great many ways to inspire a man with true Christian sentiment, and I must say that the least of them is sitting down and quoting a text from Scripture. Religious men and women have visited me in prison who have never mentioned religion, but have had the strongest influence over me. Their sincerity and conduct appealed to one more strongly than the bare Scripture. I can see in imagination now one whom I have so often seen in reality while in prison. She was a true, sweet, lovely, Christian young lady. I remember once asking her if all the people of her church were as good as she was. She replied, honestly and straightforwardly: "No; you will not find them all so liberal toward their unfortunate brothers, and every church has its share of hypocrites—mine the same as others. But God and the church remain just the same." There are some don'ts I would call to your attention. One of them is, don't try to get rich too quickly by grasping every bait thrown out to the unwary. I have been in the society of the fellows who tried to get rich quickly for the past twenty-five years, and for the most part they are a poor lot. I do not know but that I would reverse Milton's lines so as to read:

> "'Tis better to sit with a fool in Paradise
> Than some of those wise ones in prison."

Don't resort to idleness. The boy who wears out the seat of his trousers holding down dry-goods boxes on the street corners will never be president of the United States. The farmer who drives to town for pleasure several days in the week will soon have his farm advertised for sale. An idle man is sure to go into the hands of a receiver. My friends, glorious opportunities are before us, with the republic's free institutions at your command. Science and knowledge have unlocked their vaults wherein poverty and wealth are not classified—a fitting theater where the master mind shall play the leading role.

And now, with your permission, I will close with a bit of verse from Reno, the famous poet-scout. His lines are the embodiment of human nature as it should be, and to me they are a sort of creed. He says:

"I never like to see a man a-wrestling with the dumps,
　'Cause in the game of life he doesn't always catch the
　　　trumps,
　But I can always cotton to a free-and-easy cuss
　As takes his dose and thanks the Lord it wasn't any wuss.
　There ain't no use of swearin' and cussin' at your luck,
　'Cause you can't correct your troubles more than you can
　　　drown a duck.
　Remember that when beneath the load your suffering head
　　　is bowed
　That God will sprinkle sunshine in the trail of every cloud.
　If you should see a fellow man with trouble's flag unfurled,
　And lookin' like he didn't have a friend in all the world,
　Go up and slap him on the back and holler, 'How'd you do?'
　And grasp his hand so warm he'll know he has a friend in you,
　An' ask him what's a-hurtin' him, and laugh his cares away,
　An' tell him that the darkest hour is just before the day.
　Don't talk in graveyard palaver, but say it right out loud,
　That God will sprinkle sunshine in the trail of every cloud.

This world at best is but a hash of pleasures and of pain;
Some days are bright and sunny, and some are sloshed with
    rain;
An' that's jes' how it ought to be, so when the clouds roll by
We'll know jes' how to 'preciate the bright and smilin' sky.
So learn to take things as they come, and don't sweat at the
    pores
Because the Lord's opinion doesn't coincide with yours;
But always keep rememberin', when cares your path en-
    shroud,
That God has lots of sunshine to spill behind the cloud."

AN AFTERWORD

Since the foregoing was written I find that the publication of libels on myself and my dead brothers continues. The New York publishers of "five-cent-dreadfuls" are the worst offenders. One of them has published two books since my release from prison, in one of which my brothers and I are accused of the M., K. & T. train robbery at Big Springs, and in the other of the Chicago & Alton robbery at the Missouri Pacific crossing near Independence, Mo.

We had been in Stillwater prison nearly a year when the Big Springs robbery was committed, it being in September, 1877. I forget the date of the Alton robbery, but that branch of the Alton was not built until after we were sent to Stillwater, so we can not be reasonably accused of that.

———

For the portraits of my old guerrilla comrades, of whom authentic likenesses are, at this late day, hard to find, I am especially indebted to Mr. Albert Winner, of Kansas City, whose valuable collection of war pictures was kindly placed at my disposal.

COLE YOUNGER.

THE GREAT

Cole Younger
and Frank James

HISTORICAL

Wild West Show

NOW EN ROUTE

The Finest Exhibition of its Class in History

The Charge of the Rough Riders,

The Frontier as It Was,

Indian Warfare, Illustrated by Real Red-Skins,

Dare-Devil Horsemanship,

Marvelous Marksmanship,

The Perils of the Plains.

FRANK JAMES, the Scout, will personally direct every performance.

The whole under the general supervision of **COLE YOUNGER.**

H. E. ALLOTT, Manager.

Following his release from the Minnesota State Prison, Younger joined with his old comrade Frank James in a Wild West show intended to "show the frontiersman of my early manhood as he was."

Suggestions for Further Reading

MARLEY BRANT, a writer and producer in the entertainment industry, lives in Atlanta, Georgia. She is the author of:
Jesse James: The Man and the Myth. New York: Berkley Books, 1998.
The Outlaw Youngers: A Confederate Brotherhood: A Biography. Lanham, Md.: Madison Books, 1992.
Outlaws: The Illustrated History of the James-Younger Gang. Montgomery, Ala.: Elliott & Clark Publishing, 1997.

OTHER BOOKS OF RELATED INTEREST INCLUDE:

Ames, Blanche Butler, comp. *Chronicles from the Nineteenth Century: Family Letters of Blanche Butler and Adelbert Ames, Married July 21st, 1870.* 2 vols. [Clinton? Mass.], 1957. For the Northfield bank raid, see vol. 2, p. 403–6, 410, 425.

Bronaugh, W. C. *The Youngers' Fight for Freedom: A Southern Soldier's Twenty Years' Campaign to Open Northern Prison Doors—With Anecdotes of War Days.* Columbia, Mo.: Printed for the author by E. W. Stephens Publishing Company, 1906.

Cantrell, Dallas. *Youngers' Fatal Blunder: Northfield, Minnesota.* San Antonio, Tex.: Naylor Co., 1973.

Croy, Homer. *Cole Younger: Last of the Great Outlaws.* 1956. Reprinted with an introduction by Richard E. Meyer. Lincoln: University of Nebraska Press, Bison Books, 1999.

———. *Jesse James Was My Neighbor.* 1949. Reprinted with an introduction by Richard E. Meyer. Lincoln: University of Nebraska Press, Bison Books, 1997.

Hanson, J. H. *The Northfield Tragedy; or, The Raid of the Younger-James Bros. Band of Desperadoes on the Bank at Northfield, Minn.* St. Paul: J. J. Lemon, 1881.

Heilbron, W. C. *Convict Life at the Minnesota State Prison, Stillwater, Minnesota.* 1909. Updated and expanded ed. Stillwater, Minn.: Valley History Press, 1996. Includes "Real Facts about the Northfield, Minnesota, Bank Robbery," by Cole Younger, p. 130–48.

Huntington, *George. Robber and Hero: The Story of the Northfield Bank Raid.* 1895. Reprinted with an introduction by John McGuigan. St. Paul: Minnesota Historical Society Press, Borealis Books, 1986.

Koblas, John. *The Jesse James Northfield Raid: Confessions of the Ninth Man.* St. Cloud, Minn.: North Star Press of St. Cloud, 1999.

Leslie, Edward E. *The Devil Knows How to Ride: The True Story of William Clarke Quantrill and His Confederate Raiders.* New York: Random House, 1996.

Settle, William A., Jr. *Jesse James Was His Name: or, Fact and Fiction Concerning the Careers of the Notorious James Brothers of Missouri.* 1966. Reprint. Lincoln: University of Nebraska Press, Bison Books, 1977.

Trenerry, Walter N. *Murder in Minnesota: A Collection of True Cases.* St. Paul: Minnesota Historical Society Press, 1962. Includes the murders of Joseph Lee Heywood and Nicholas Gustavson during the Northfield bank raid, p. 85–105.

Printed in the USA
CPSIA information can be obtained
at www.ICGtesting.com
JSHW082212140824
68134JS00014B/573